# Daily Wisdom

*Islamic Prayers &*
*Supplications*

Abdur Raheem Kidwai

**KUBE**
PUBLISHING

*Daily Wisdom: Islamic Prayers and Supplications*

First published in England by

**Kube Publishing Ltd**
Markfield Conference Centre
Ratby Lane, Markfield,
Leicestershire LE67 9SY
United Kingdom
Tel: +44 (0) 1530 249230
Fax: +44 (0) 1530 249656
Website: www.kubepublishing.com
Email: info@kubepublishing.com

Cataloguing-in-Publication Data
is available from the British Library

ISBN 978-1-84774-043-4 *casebound*
ISBN 978-1-84774-048-9 *casebound (deluxe edition with slipcase)*

*Book Design*: Imtiaz Manjra
*Book typesetting*: nqaddoura@hotmail.com
Printed by Imak Offset, Turkey

# CONTENTS

## KEY TO ABBREVIATIONS

The following abbreviations have been used in this book to indicate the sources of the quoted Prophetic petitionary prayers and supplications, which are either to the compilers or titles of the collections of Hadith. Full references are given in the bibliographies at the end.

A = Ahmad, *Musnad*
AD = Abu Dawud, *Sunan*
B = Bukhari, *Sahih*
BA = Bukhari, *Adab al-Mufrad*
H = Hakim, *al-Mustadrak*
Hy = Al-Haythami, *Majma' al-Zawa'id*
IAS = Ibn Abi Shaybah, *al-Musannaf*
IM = Ibn Majah, *Sunan*
IS = Ibn Sunni, *'Amal al-Yawm wa al-Layla*
M = Muslim, *Sahih*
N = Al-Nawawi, *al-Adhkar*
S = Al-Shawkani, *Nayl al-Awtar*
T = Al-Tirmidhi, *Sunan*
TbD = Al-Tabarani, *Du'a'*
TbMA = Al-Tabarani, *al-Mu'jam al-Awsat*
TbMK = Al-Tabarani, *al-Mu'jam al-Kabir*
TT = Al-Mundhiri, *al-Targhib wa al-Tarhib*

# PREFACE

This work presents an anthology of prayers and supplications selected from the Qur'an and the Prophetic Tradition (*Hadith*). In Islam, prayers have a special place, a point which is further elaborated in the 'Introduction' to this work. In all, it contains 366 brief yet comprehensive prayers and supplications which have been arranged thematically. It should enable you, the reader, to recite a prayer a day throughout the year or to select a prayer relevant to your needs. It will encourage you to forge and strengthen your ties with your Creator and Lord. The prayers and supplications here will also bless you with emotional and spiritual relief and tranquillity, and they will help you to overcome difficulties and to improve your state of affairs with God's grace and permission.

This work is the latest addition to the *Daily Wisdom* series brought out by Kube Publishing for the benefit of those interested in gaining knowledge of the basic articles of faith and main teachings of Islam in accessible English. This selection provides you with an opportunity to engage in a moment of daily reflection. The earlier titles in this series contain selections from texts of the Qur'an and

*Hadith*. This collection will aid in the learning and recitation of and reflection upon a range of supplications which are needed in our everyday lives. These supplications address the human condition – of seeking favours from God, His protection and forgiveness, and His help in the concerns of everyday life, His guidance, and, above all, His pleasure that ensures joy and success in this world and the Next.

I am thankful to Yahya Birt, Commissioning Editor at Kube Publishing for having entrusted this assignment to me and for his valuable suggestions about the tenor of this work. I must also thank Haris Ahmad, Executive Director of Kube Publishing, for his support.

**Abdur Raheem Kidwai**
Aligarh Muslim University, India
Rabiʿ al-Awwal 1433 H
February 2012 CE

*In the name of God, Most Compassionate
and Most Merciful*

# INTRODUCTION

*Your Lord says: 'Pray to me, and I will accept your prayers.'*

al-Mu'min 40:60

*Call upon your Lord with humility and in private.*
al-A'raf 7:55

The above quoted Qur'anic verses underscore the pivotal role of *du'a'* (supplication or petitionary prayer) in Islam. Many supplications appear in the Qur'an with a view to instructing humanity on how to supplicate to God. In Islam, supplications occupy the pride of place. The human being as God's servant and being fully dependent on Him should turn to Him for everything and by the same token express thanks for all that he has. This is an integral part of devotional worship in Islam. Significantly enough, the opening chapter (*surah*) of the Qur'an, al-Fatihah, which every Muslim is obliged to recite in the five daily compulsory prayers represents the spirit and tenor of supplication. Take the following verses of this *surah* as illustrative.

*Guide us to the straight way, the way of those whom You have favoured, not the way of those who have incurred Your wrath, nor of those who have gone astray.*

(al-Fatihah 1:6-7)

As the Prophet (may God bless him and grant him peace) succinctly put it: 'The supplication represents the essence of worship', for it marks direct communion between God and His servant. A striking feature of supplication in Islam is that it does not involve any intermediary. Moreover, it is an emotionally and spiritually fulfilling exercise. Even when our supplications are not granted, the act itself brings immense comfort and solace. For it provides us with an opportunity to turn wholly and humbly to our Lord. We invoke God from the depths of our hearts and in a spirit of total self-surrender to Him.

Making supplications serves as a constant reminder of our servitude to God, of our total dependence on Him for everything – big or small. We become all the more aware of our inadequacies and failings, which spur us to strive harder for our moral and spiritual development. Our reliance on God in every aspect of our lives and our utter helplessness are to the fore in this exemplary Qur'anic supplication:

*Our Lord! Do not take us to task, if we forget or err. Do not place on us a burden such as You placed on those before us. Our Lord! Do not impose on us that for which we do not have strength. And pardon us, forgive us, and have mercy on us. You are our Lord, so make us triumph over the unbelievers.*

(al-Baqarah 2:286)

We are liable to err and to forget Divine guidance. What is, however, more important is that we should be conscious of this weakness and repent as soon as we realize the lapses we have committed. Islam does not presuppose that we are infallible creatures like the angels, incapable of any wrong, but instead teaches us that when we slip, we should turn to the All-Merciful in repentance. If, in Islam it is a credal truth that the prophets and messengers of God are divinely protected from intentional wrongdoing, the Qur'an records their inadvertent lapses from which they always repented and sought God's forgiveness as an example to us. The above supplication thus teaches us this fundamental truth about sin and Divine forgiveness. We should never ask God to put us to any test for it might prove too hard for us to overcome temptation or suffering.

Another Qur'anic supplication, made by the Prophet Abraham (peace and blessings be upon him), is worth remembering at all times. For it reminds us of our basic religious duty and of our ultimate end:

> *O my Lord! Make me one who establishes regular Prayer, and also raise such among my children, O our Lord. And accept my supplication.*
>
> *O our Lord! Cover us with Your forgiveness – me, my parents and all the believers on the Day of Reckoning.*
>
> (Ibrahim 14:40-41)

Prayer is the cornerstone of the Islamic faith, shown by the emphasis given to it in the Prophet Abraham's supplication. Sincerity consists in desiring for others what we like best for ourselves. Accordingly, the supplication extends to our children as well for they too should be particular about offering prayer regularly. It is God Who enables us to perform this important religious duty on which our success in both worlds depends. Therefore, God's forgiveness in this supplication is especially invoked. It is equally important to attain His forgiveness and mercy through which our lapses may be overlooked. The universality of Islam is evident from this supplication. For Divine forgiveness is sought for not only for our parents but also for all Muslims. This will secure salvation for us on the Day of Judgement. Concern for the Hereafter should be constantly present in our hearts and minds, for it helps us to follow the straight path steadily and to shun sin. The Qur'an teaches us:

> *And if you are prompted by a provocation from Satan, seek refuge with God. He, and He alone, is All-Hearing, All-Knowing.*
> (Ha Mim al-Sajdah 41:36)

That making supplication is the bulwark of the believers is emphasized in the Prophetic tradition. We turn to God in both prosperity and adversity. It is the best means for us to forge, maintain and strengthen our link with our Creator, Sustainer and Lord. We constantly stand in need of Him to meet our material, emotional and spiritual needs. It should not therefore come as a surprise that the Qur'an contains several prayers made fervently by the prophets, seeking God's help to fulfil their human needs, such as having a child, seeking recovery from sickness or asking for increase in knowledge. Some of these prayers are included in this anthology.

Not only did the Prophet Muhammad (may God bless him and grant him peace) often make supplications to God with the utmost fervour and humility, but he also exhorted his Companions to do the same. A representative supplication on the Prophet's authority is cited below:

O my Lord! Keep me firm in my faith, for
it is my only defence. Grant me good in the
world in which I earn my bread. Improve my
prospects in the Next World, to which I have
to ultimately return. Make my life a blessing
and my death an escape from evil.

(Muslim, *Bab Fadl al-Tahlil wa al-Du'a'*)

Needless to add, this supplication takes into
account both worlds and seeks the best in both.
As long as we are alive, we should keep on adding
good deeds to our credit and seek to have a
good death such that we do not fall into some
temptation or evil at the moment of our inevitable
demise. Both life and death should thus be
characterized by good. While the focus is on the
Next World, the concerns of this life, especially of
one's livelihood, are not neglected. Islam represents
the perfect amalgam of both this and that world.
A Muslim is not expected to lead a solitary life,
neglecting his or her obligations towards one's
parents, spouse or children, community or fellow
human beings at large. Yet a Muslim should not
be engrossed in worldly pursuits at the expense of
disregarding the Hereafter.

Some other equally important concerns find men-
tion in the following supplication taught by the
Prophet (may God bless him and grant him peace):

O our Lord! Infuse mutual love into our
hearts and improve our social relations.
Guide us to the way of safety and deliver us
from darkness into light. Protect us against
all indecency and obscenity, both manifest
and hidden. Bless our hearing, seeing, hearts,
children and wives. Accept our repentance.
Surely You are the One Who pardons. You
are Most Merciful. Enable us to thank You
for Your favours: make us deserving of them
and bestow all of them upon us.

(*Kanz al-'Ummal*)

Cordial social relations are essential for a happy,
peaceful life for individuals and society at large.
The above supplication underscores the same in
invoking God for this blessing. Divine guidance is
of immense value to us, for it directs us to lead life
in the best way and ensures our eternal success in
the Next Life. Taking the cue from *Surah al-Fatihah,*
which presses home the same point of being
blessed with Divine guidance, God has bestowed
mental and physical faculties on everyone.
Likewise, everyone enjoys a family life. However
all these gifts must be used in the light of God's
guidance. For example, if the faculties of speech,
hearing and sight are abused, these are worse
than a curse for us. For their abuse lands us in
the Hellfire. By the same token, if we deviate from
the moral code and religious law (*Shari'ah*) in our

overflowing love for our spouses and children, then this too can spell eternal damnation. We should, of course, meet their needs and demands with love and kindness. However, if we resort to unlawful means to meet their needs, then this amounts to hurling ourselves into the Hellfire. Accordingly, the above supplication teaches us to solicit Divine help on this important count. We should make a point of thanking God for His numerous favours and turn to Him in sincere repentance to obtain His forgiveness. So, making supplications serves many purposes and is an integral part of the Islamic way of life.

The following norms should be followed while presenting prayers before God. One should do so in a state of ritual purity, after making ritual purification (*wudu'*). This infuses into us greater God-consciousness and washes away our sins if *wudu'* is performed correctly and with the right motivation. Likewise, we should face the direction of Makkah (the *qiblah*) when supplicating. Needless to say, God is not confined to any particular direction. However, the above practice helps the supplicant to focus. While supplicating, we should raise and cup our hands, as a gesture of seeking some favour from God. Conversely, when we pray to avert some calamity, we should turn our palms face downwards. Each prayer should be prefaced and interlaced with words that glorify God's greatness, uniqueness and supremacy. It should preferably conclude with sending peace and blessings upon the Prophet (*salawat* or *durud*). The supplication or petitionary prayer (*du'a'*) should be characterized by the utmost humility, a low tone of voice, sincerity of purpose, and sure conviction. If these things are not present, then we would do better to supplicate again. Crying while baring our souls before our Creator is highly recommended, although it is not a condition for sincerity of purpose, which can take many forms. We should be forthright in confessing our lapses and sins and fervently request God for forgiveness. Our repentance should include giving up completely the sin or wrong committed by us, expressing our genuine remorse over having committed that wrong, and our resolving not to engage in that or any other wrong again. Our prayer should not even imply a curse upon anyone. A victim may, however, request that God either guides or punishes the guilty. While praying for our prosperity, salvation or for anything good, we should request that fellow Muslims get the same blessings too. We should also pray for the salvation and guidance of all humanity.

While we may offer supplications at any time and in any place that is wholesome and clean, some

Prophetic traditions identify special sites and hours for the acceptance of supplications. Some of these traditions indicate also what kind of person is more likely to have his or her supplications granted. Nonetheless, out of His sheer generosity and compassion, God may accept anyone's supplication made anywhere as it pleases Him.

The Prophet (may God bless him and grant him peace) is on record having stated that the supplicant who shuns major sins, earns a lawful income and is pious may receive God's greater attention. Likewise, the supplications of parents for their children and *vice versa* may be more readily granted in view of the special bond of love and affection between them. Supplications by a traveller, by one who is fasting and by one who is performing the greater or lesser pilgrimages to Makkah (Hajj or 'Umrah respectively) or struggling morally for the cause of God (the greater Jihad) may also merit priority. The supplication of any wronged or victimised person that justice is served to the perpetrator readily reaches God and may get an immediate response.

The best way to supplicate to God is in prostration, for this underscores our total submission, both literal and metaphorical, to Him and our earnestness in seeking some favour from Him. A supplication is especially auspicious when made in the small hours of night, that is, at *Tahajjud* time, at the time of breaking the fast, on Fridays, on the Night of Power (*Laylat al-Qadr*) during the month of fasting in Ramadan, on the day of ʿArafah at the conclusion of the Hajj, at the conclusion of our daily prayers, while drinking Zamzam water, inside the great mosque in Makkah and at all the sacred sites associated with Hajj. Tradition records these and many other special times, occasions and places.

Notwithstanding these special times and places which may contribute to the acceptance of supplications, our utmost sincerity and devotion to God and our conviction that He answers our supplications as befits His mercy and wisdom is what really counts. He may answer our prayers directly, or grant us something better than what we have asked for. Even if a supplication is not granted, we must believe that its rejection was either to avert some unforeseen harm that its granting may have brought upon us or that God may compensate us in the Next Life rather than in this one. How comforting and consoling is this truth conveyed to us by the Prophet (may God bless him and grant him peace)!

# Daily Wisdom

*Qur'anic Prayers &*
*Supplications*

**DAY 1**

All praise is for Allah, the Lord of the entire universe. He is Most Compassionate, Most Merciful. He is the Master of the Day of Judgement. You alone we worship, and from You alone do we seek help. Guide us to the straight way, the way of those whom You have blessed, not of those who invite Your wrath [because of their evil actions], nor of those who have lost the [straight] way.

(al-Fatihah 1:1-7)

**DAY 2**

Our Lord, accept this from us. Surely You are All-Hearing, All-Knowing.

(al-Baqarah 2:127)

ٱلْحَمْدُ لِلَّهِ رَبِّ ٱلْعَٰلَمِينَ ۝ ٱلرَّحْمَٰنِ ٱلرَّحِيمِ ۝ مَٰلِكِ يَوْمِ ٱلدِّينِ ۝ إِيَّاكَ نَعْبُدُ وَإِيَّاكَ نَسْتَعِينُ ۝ ٱهْدِنَا ٱلصِّرَٰطَ ٱلْمُسْتَقِيمَ ۝ صِرَٰطَ ٱلَّذِينَ أَنْعَمْتَ عَلَيْهِمْ غَيْرِ ٱلْمَغْضُوبِ عَلَيْهِمْ وَلَا ٱلضَّآلِّينَ ۝

(الفاتحة ١:١-٧)

... رَبَّنَا تَقَبَّلْ مِنَّآ إِنَّكَ أَنتَ ٱلسَّمِيعُ ٱلْعَلِيمُ ۝

(البقرة ٢: ١٢٧)

**DAY 3**

O our Lord, make us and our children obedient to You. Show us the ways of worshipping You, and turn to us in mercy. Surely You are Most Forgiving, Most Merciful. O our Lord, send to them [our future generations] a Messenger from among them who will recite Your signs to them, instruct them in the Book and wisdom, and purify them. Surely You are Almighty, the Wisest.

(al-Baqarah 2:128-129)

**DAY 4**

We believe in Allah and in what is sent to us and to Abraham, Ishmael, Isaac, Jacob and the children of Jacob. We believe in what was given to Moses, Jesus and the Prophets by their Lord. We do not make any distinction among them. We submit to Allah.

(al-Baqarah 2:136)

اليوم
٣

رَبَّنَا وَٱجْعَلْنَا مُسْلِمَيْنِ لَكَ وَمِن ذُرِّيَّتِنَآ أُمَّةً مُّسْلِمَةً لَّكَ وَأَرِنَا مَنَاسِكَنَا وَتُبْ عَلَيْنَآ إِنَّكَ أَنتَ ٱلتَّوَّابُ ٱلرَّحِيمُ ۝ رَبَّنَا وَٱبْعَثْ فِيهِمْ رَسُولًا مِّنْهُمْ يَتْلُوا۟ عَلَيْهِمْ ءَايَٰتِكَ وَيُعَلِّمُهُمُ ٱلْكِتَٰبَ وَٱلْحِكْمَةَ وَيُزَكِّيهِمْ إِنَّكَ أَنتَ ٱلْعَزِيزُ ٱلْحَكِيمُ ۝

(البقرة ٢: ١٢٨-١٢٩)

اليوم
٤

... ءَامَنَّا بِٱللَّهِ وَمَآ أُنزِلَ إِلَيْنَا وَمَآ أُنزِلَ إِلَىٰٓ إِبْرَٰهِـۧمَ وَإِسْمَـٰعِيلَ وَإِسْحَٰقَ وَيَعْقُوبَ وَٱلْأَسْبَاطِ وَمَآ أُوتِىَ مُوسَىٰ وَعِيسَىٰ وَمَآ أُوتِىَ ٱلنَّبِيُّونَ مِن رَّبِّهِمْ لَا نُفَرِّقُ بَيْنَ أَحَدٍ مِّنْهُمْ وَنَحْنُ لَهُۥ مُسْلِمُونَ ۝

(البقرة ٢: ١٣٦)

**DAY**
**5**

We belong to Allah and to Him is [our] return.

(al-Baqarah 2:156)

**DAY**
**6**

Our Lord, give us good in this world and good in the Next Life, and save us from the Hellfire.

(al-Baqarah 2:201)

**اليوم**
**٥**

... إِنَّا لِلَّهِ وَإِنَّا إِلَيْهِ رَاجِعُونَ ۝

(البقرة ١٥٦:٢)

**اليوم**
**٦**

... رَبَّنَآ ءَاتِنَا فِى ٱلدُّنْيَا حَسَنَةً وَفِى ٱلْأَخِرَةِ حَسَنَةً وَقِنَا
عَذَابَ ٱلنَّارِ ۝

(البقرة ٢٠١:٢)

**DAY 7**

Our Lord, shower us with patience and set our feet firm, and grant us victory over the unbelieving people.

(al-Baqarah 2:250)

**DAY 8**

Allah is Ever-Living, Self-Subsisting. There is no god besides Him. Neither slumber nor sleep overtakes Him. His is all that is in the heavens and all that is on earth. Who can intercede with Him, except with His permission? He knows what lies before and behind His creatures. They cannot encompass anything of His knowledge, except what He wills. His throne extends over the heavens and the earth. He feels no fatigue in guarding these. He is Most High, Most Glorious.

(al-Baqarah 2:255)

اليوم
٧

... رَبَّنَآ أَفْرِغْ عَلَيْنَا صَبْرًا وَثَبِّتْ أَقْدَامَنَا وَانصُرْنَا عَلَى ٱلْقَوْمِ
ٱلْكَٰفِرِينَ ۝

(البقرة ٢: ٢٥٠)

اليوم
٨

ٱللَّهُ لَآ إِلَٰهَ إِلَّا هُوَ ٱلْحَىُّ ٱلْقَيُّومُ لَا تَأْخُذُهُۥ سِنَةٌ وَلَا نَوْمٌ
لَّهُۥ مَا فِى ٱلسَّمَٰوَٰتِ وَمَا فِى ٱلْأَرْضِ مَن ذَا ٱلَّذِى
يَشْفَعُ عِندَهُۥٓ إِلَّا بِإِذْنِهِۦ يَعْلَمُ مَا بَيْنَ أَيْدِيهِمْ وَمَا خَلْفَهُمْ
وَلَا يُحِيطُونَ بِشَىْءٍ مِّنْ عِلْمِهِۦٓ إِلَّا بِمَا شَآءَ وَسِعَ
كُرْسِيُّهُ ٱلسَّمَٰوَٰتِ وَٱلْأَرْضَ وَلَا يَـُٔودُهُۥ حِفْظُهُمَا وَهُوَ
ٱلْعَلِىُّ ٱلْعَظِيمُ ۝

(البقرة ٢: ٢٥٥)

**DAY 9**

We do not make any distinction among any of Allah's Messengers. We hear and obey. Our Lord, grant us Your forgiveness. To You is the return.

(al-Baqarah 2:285)

**DAY 10**

O our Lord, do not take us to task if we forget or make mistakes. O our Lord, do not place on us a burden which You had laid on those before us. O our Lord, do not place on us a burden which we cannot bear. Overlook our mistakes and forgive us. Have mercy on us. You are our Protector. Help us against the unbelieving people.

(al-Baqarah 2:286)

اليوم
٩

... لَا نُفَرِّقُ بَيْنَ أَحَدٍ مِّن رُّسُلِهِۦ وَقَالُوا۟ سَمِعْنَا وَأَطَعْنَا غُفْرَانَكَ رَبَّنَا وَإِلَيْكَ ٱلْمَصِيرُ ۝

(البقرة: ٢٨٥:٢)

اليوم
١٠

... رَبَّنَا لَا تُؤَاخِذْنَا إِن نَّسِينَا أَوْ أَخْطَأْنَا رَبَّنَا وَلَا تَحْمِلْ عَلَيْنَا إِصْرًا كَمَا حَمَلْتَهُۥ عَلَى ٱلَّذِينَ مِن قَبْلِنَا رَبَّنَا وَلَا تُحَمِّلْنَا مَا لَا طَاقَةَ لَنَا بِهِۦ وَٱعْفُ عَنَّا وَٱغْفِرْ لَنَا وَٱرْحَمْنَا أَنتَ مَوْلَىٰنَا فَٱنصُرْنَا عَلَى ٱلْقَوْمِ ٱلْكَـٰفِرِينَ ۝

(البقرة: ٢٨٦:٢)

11

**DAY 11**

O our Lord, do not let our hearts turn away after You have shown us the straight way. Grant us Your mercy, for You grant blessings generously. O our Lord, You will certainly gather all people on the Day of Judgement about which there is no doubt. Allah does not break His promise.

(Al 'Imran 3:8-9)

**DAY 12**

O our Lord, we indeed believe. So forgive our sins and save us from the Hellfire.

(Al 'Imran 3:16)

رَبَّنَا لَا تُزِغْ قُلُوبَنَا بَعْدَ إِذْ هَدَيْتَنَا وَهَبْ لَنَا مِن لَّدُنكَ رَحْمَةً إِنَّكَ أَنتَ ٱلْوَهَّابُ ۝ رَبَّنَآ إِنَّكَ جَامِعُ ٱلنَّاسِ لِيَوْمٍ لَّا رَيْبَ فِيهِ إِنَّ ٱللَّهَ لَا يُخْلِفُ ٱلْمِيعَادَ ۝

(آل عمران ٣: ٨-٩)

... رَبَّنَآ إِنَّنَآ ءَامَنَّا فَٱغْفِرْ لَنَا ذُنُوبَنَا وَقِنَا عَذَابَ ٱلنَّارِ ۝

(آل عمران ٣: ١٦)

DAY
13

Allah, Lord of power! You grant power to whom You like and You take away power from whom You like. You honour whom You like and You degrade whom You like. All good is in Your hand. You have power over everything. You cause the night to pass into the day and You cause the day to pass into the night. You bring the living out of the dead and You bring the dead out of the living. You grant provision beyond measure to whom You like.

(Al 'Imran 3:26-27)

DAY
14

O my Lord, I dedicate to You what is in my womb for Your service alone. So accept it from me. You are All-Hearing, All-Knowing.

(Al 'Imran 3:35)

... ٱللَّهُمَّ مَـٰلِكَ ٱلْمُلْكِ تُؤْتِى ٱلْمُلْكَ مَن تَشَآءُ وَتَنزِعُ ٱلْمُلْكَ مِمَّن تَشَآءُ وَتُعِزُّ مَن تَشَآءُ وَتُذِلُّ مَن تَشَآءُ بِيَدِكَ ٱلْخَيْرُ إِنَّكَ عَلَىٰ كُلِّ شَىْءٍ قَدِيرٌ ۝ تُولِجُ ٱلَّيْلَ فِى ٱلنَّهَارِ وَتُولِجُ ٱلنَّهَارَ فِى ٱلَّيْلِ وَتُخْرِجُ ٱلْحَىَّ مِنَ ٱلْمَيِّتِ وَتُخْرِجُ ٱلْمَيِّتَ مِنَ ٱلْحَىِّ وَتَرْزُقُ مَن تَشَآءُ بِغَيْرِ حِسَابٍ ۝

(آل عمران ٣: ٢٦-٢٧)

... رَبِّ إِنِّى نَذَرْتُ لَكَ مَا فِى بَطْنِى مُحَرَّرًا فَتَقَبَّلْ مِنِّى إِنَّكَ أَنتَ ٱلسَّمِيعُ ٱلْعَلِيمُ ۝

(آل عمران ٣: ٣٥)

**DAY**
**15**

*O* my Lord, grant me out of Your grace a good child. You hear all prayers.

(Al 'Imran 3:38)

**DAY**
**16**

*O* our Lord, we believe in what You have revealed and we obey the Messenger. Make us those who endorse (the truth).

(Al 'Imran 3:53)

رَبِّ هَبْ لِي مِن لَّدُنكَ ذُرِّيَّةً طَيِّبَةً إِنَّكَ سَمِيعُ ٱلدُّعَاءِ ﴿٣٨﴾...

(آل عمران ٣:٣٨)

رَبَّنَآ ءَامَنَّا بِمَآ أَنزَلْتَ وَٱتَّبَعْنَا ٱلرَّسُولَ فَٱكْتُبْنَا مَعَ ٱلشَّٰهِدِينَ ﴿٥٣﴾

(آل عمران ٣:٥٣)

17

**DAY 17**

O our Lord, forgive our sins, and our excesses in our dealings. Keep our feet firm and help us against the unbelieving people.

(Al 'Imran 3:147)

**DAY 18**

A llah is enough for us, and He is an excellent Guardian.

(Al 'Imran 3:173)

... رَبَّنَا اغْفِرْ لَنَا ذُنُوبَنَا وَإِسْرَافَنَا فِي أَمْرِنَا وَثَبِّتْ أَقْدَامَنَا

وَانصُرْنَا عَلَى الْقَوْمِ الْكَٰفِرِينَ ۝

(آل عمران ٣: ١٤٧)

... حَسْبُنَا اللَّهُ وَنِعْمَ الْوَكِيلُ ۝

(آل عمران ٣: ١٧٣)

**DAY 19**

O our Lord, You have not created all this without a purpose. Glory be to You. Save us from the punishment of the Hellfire.

(Al 'Imran 3:191)

**DAY 20**

O our Lord, he whom You throw into the Hellfire stands disgraced. There will be no helper for the wrongdoers.

(Al 'Imran 3:192)

رَبَّنَا مَا خَلَقْتَ هَذَا بَاطِلًا سُبْحَنَكَ فَقِنَا عَذَابَ ٱلنَّارِ ۝

(آل عمران ٣: ١٩١)

رَبَّنَآ إِنَّكَ مَن تُدْخِلِ ٱلنَّارَ فَقَدْ أَخْزَيْتَهُۥ وَمَا لِلظَّلِمِينَ مِنْ أَنصَارٍ ۝

(آل عمران ٣: ١٩٢)

**DAY 21**

O our Lord, we heard a person calling to faith, saying – 'Believe in your Lord' – so we believed. O our Lord, forgive our sins, wipe out our evil deeds and cause us to die in the manner of the pious.

(Al 'Imran 3:193)

**DAY 22**

O our Lord, grant us what You have promised us through Your Messengers, and do not humiliate us on the Day of Judgement; indeed, You do not break Your promise.

(Al 'Imran 3:194)

رَبَّنَآ إِنَّنَا سَمِعْنَا مُنَادِيًا يُنَادِى لِلْإِيمَـٰنِ أَنْ ءَامِنُواْ بِرَبِّكُمْ فَـَامَنَّاۚ رَبَّنَا فَٱغْفِرْ لَنَا ذُنُوبَنَا وَكَفِّرْ عَنَّا سَيِّـَٔاتِنَا وَتَوَفَّنَا مَعَ ٱلْأَبْرَارِ ﴿١٩٣﴾

(آل عمران ٣: ١٩٣)

رَبَّنَا وَءَاتِنَا مَا وَعَدتَّنَا عَلَىٰ رُسُلِكَ وَلَا تُخْزِنَا يَوْمَ ٱلْقِيَـٰمَةِۖ إِنَّكَ لَا تُخْلِفُ ٱلْمِيعَادَ ﴿١٩٤﴾

(آل عمران ٣: ١٩٤)

**DAY 23**

*O* our Lord, take us out of this land: its people are unjust. Raise for us a protector from Yourself, and raise for us a helper from Yourself.

(al-Nisa' 4:75)

**DAY 24**

*O* our Lord, we do believe: so write us down with those who endorse [the truth]. And why should we not believe in Allah and in the truth which has come down to us when we long that our Lord should include us among the pious?

(al-Ma'idah 5:83-84)

... رَبَّنَآ أَخْرِجْنَا مِنْ هَـٰذِهِ ٱلْقَرْيَةِ ٱلظَّالِمِ أَهْلُهَا وَٱجْعَل لَّنَا مِن لَّدُنكَ وَلِيًّا وَٱجْعَل لَّنَا مِن لَّدُنكَ نَصِيرًا ۝

(النساء ٤: ٧٥)

... رَبَّنَآ ءَامَنَّا فَٱكْتُبْنَا مَعَ ٱلشَّـٰهِدِينَ ۝ وَمَا لَنَا لَا نُؤْمِنُ بِٱللَّهِ وَمَا جَآءَنَا مِنَ ٱلْحَقِّ وَنَطْمَعُ أَن يُدْخِلَنَا رَبُّنَا مَعَ ٱلْقَوْمِ ٱلصَّـٰلِحِينَ ۝

(المائدة ٥: ٨٣-٨٤)

Allah, our Lord, send down to us a table [full of food] from the heavens that it may be a festival for us, for the first and the last of us, and a sign from You. And provide for us, for You are the best of providers.

(al-Ma'idah 5:114)

DAY
26

 our Lord, we have wronged our souls. If You do not forgive us and have mercy on us, we will be among those who are lost.

(al-A'raf 7:23)

اَللَّهُمَّ رَبَّنَآ أَنزِلْ عَلَيْنَا مَآئِدَةً مِّنَ ٱلسَّمَآءِ تَكُونُ لَنَا عِيدًا لِّأَوَّلِنَا وَءَاخِرِنَا وَءَايَةً مِّنكَ ۖ وَٱرْزُقْنَا وَأَنتَ خَيْرُ ٱلرَّٰزِقِينَ ۝

(المائدة ٥: ١١٤)

رَبَّنَا ظَلَمْنَآ أَنفُسَنَا وَإِن لَّمْ تَغْفِرْ لَنَا وَتَرْحَمْنَا لَنَكُونَنَّ مِنَ ٱلْخَٰسِرِينَ ۝

(الأعراف ٧: ٢٣)

**DAY 27**

ll praise be to Allah Who guided us to this: had He not guided us, we would never have found the [straight] way.

(al-A'raf 7:43)

**DAY 28**

ur Lord has knowledge of all things. In Allah we trust. O our Lord, decide the matter with truth between us and our people, for You are the best of judges.

(al-A'raf 7:89)

... ٱلْحَمْدُ لِلَّهِ ٱلَّذِى هَدَىٰنَا لِهَٰذَا وَمَا كُنَّا لِنَهْتَدِىَ لَوْلَآ أَنْ هَدَىٰنَا ٱللَّهُ ... ۝

(الأعراف ٧: ٤٣)

... وَسِعَ رَبُّنَا كُلَّ شَىْءٍ عِلْمًا عَلَى ٱللَّهِ تَوَكَّلْنَا رَبَّنَا ٱفْتَحْ بَيْنَنَا وَبَيْنَ قَوْمِنَا بِٱلْحَقِّ وَأَنتَ خَيْرُ ٱلْفَٰتِحِينَ ۝

(الأعراف ٧: ٨٩)

**DAY 29**

O our Lord, grant us steadfastness and let us die as those who are devoted to You.

(al-A'raf 7:126)

**DAY 30**

O my Lord, forgive me and my brother [the Prophet Aaron]. Admit us to Your mercy: You are Most Merciful of all those who show mercy.

(al-A'raf 7:151)

اليوم
٢٩

... رَبَّنَآ أَفۡرِغۡ عَلَيۡنَا صَبۡرًا وَتَوَفَّنَا مُسۡلِمِينَ ۝

(الأعراف ٧:١٢٦)

اليوم
٣٠

... رَبِّ ٱغۡفِرۡ لِى وَلِأَخِى وَأَدۡخِلۡنَا فِى رَحۡمَتِكَ
وَأَنتَ أَرۡحَمُ ٱلرَّٰحِمِينَ ۝

(الأعراف ٧:١٥١)

(O our Lord,) You alone are our Protector, so forgive us and have mercy on us. You are the best of those who forgive. Grant us good in this world and in the Hereafter, for we turn to You.

(al-A'raf 7:155-156)

Their [the believers'] call in it [the Garden of Bliss] will be: 'Glory be to You (O Allah)!' Their greeting there will be: 'Peace!' Their call will always end with: 'All praise be to Allah, the Lord of the universe.'

(Yunus 10:10)

اليوم
٣١

وَٱكْتُبْ لَنَا فِى هَـٰذِهِ ٱلدُّنْيَا حَسَنَةً وَفِى ٱلْآخِرَةِ
إِنَّا هُدْنَآ إِلَيْكَ ... ۝

(الأعراف ٧: ١٥٥-١٥٦)

اليوم
٣٢

دَعْوَىٰهُمْ فِيهَا سُبْحَـٰنَكَ ٱللَّهُمَّ وَتَحِيَّتُهُمْ فِيهَا سَلَـٰمٌ وَءَاخِرُ
دَعْوَىٰهُمْ أَنِ ٱلْحَمْدُ لِلَّهِ رَبِّ ٱلْعَـٰلَمِينَ ۝

(يونس ١٠: ١٠)

**DAY 33**

*O*ur Lord, do not make us a test for those who oppress; deliver us by Your mercy from those who reject [You].

(Yunus 10:85-86)

**DAY 34**

*B*oard it [the ark] in the name of Allah, as it moves or is at rest. My Lord is Most Forgiving, Most Merciful.

(Hud 11:41)

34

اليوم
٣٣

... رَبَّنَا لَا تَجْعَلْنَا فِتْنَةً لِّلْقَوْمِ ٱلظَّـٰلِمِينَ ۝ وَنَجِّنَا بِرَحْمَتِكَ مِنَ ٱلْقَوْمِ ٱلْكَـٰفِرِينَ ۝

(يونس ١٠: ٨٥-٨٦)

اليوم
٣٤

... ٱرْكَبُوا۟ فِيهَا بِسْمِ ٱللَّهِ مَجْر۪ىٰهَا وَمُرْسَىٰهَآ إِنَّ رَبِّى لَغَفُورٌ رَّحِيمٌ ۝

(هود ١١: ٤١)

**DAY
35**

O my Lord, I seek Your protection against asking for something of which I have no knowledge. If You do not forgive me and do not have mercy on me, I will be among those who are lost.

(Hud 11:47)

**DAY
36**

O my Lord, I prefer prison to what they [these women] ask me to do. If You do not turn away their mischief from me, I will draw towards them. I will be then one of the ignorant people.

(Yusuf 12:33)

... رَبِّ إِنِّيٓ أَعُوذُ بِكَ أَنۡ أَسۡئَلَكَ مَا لَيۡسَ لِى بِهِۦ عِلۡمٌ وَإِلَّا تَغۡفِرۡ لِى وَتَرۡحَمۡنِيٓ أَكُن مِّنَ ٱلۡخَٰسِرِينَ ۝

(هود ١١: ٤٧)

... رَبِّ ٱلسِّجۡنُ أَحَبُّ إِلَىَّ مِمَّا يَدۡعُونَنِىٓ إِلَيۡهِ وَإِلَّا تَصۡرِفۡ عَنِّى كَيۡدَهُنَّ أَصۡبُ إِلَيۡهِنَّ وَأَكُن مِّنَ ٱلۡجَٰهِلِينَ ۝

(يوسف ١٢: ٣٣)

Originator of the heavens and the earth, You are my Protector in this world and the Next. Let me die as a Muslim [obedient to You], and join me with the pious.

(Yusuf 12:101)

O my Lord, make this town [Makkah] one of peace and security, and keep me and my children from worshipping idols. O my Lord, these [idols] have misled many people. He who follows my way is of me; and if anyone disobeys me, then You are Most Forgiving, Most Merciful. O my Lord, I have settled some of my children in a barren valley by Your Sacred House. O our Lord, enable them to offer prayers regularly, so fill the hearts of people with love for them, and give them fruits to eat so that they may give thanks [to You].

(Ibrahim 14:35-37)

... فَاطِرَ ٱلسَّمَـٰوَٰتِ وَٱلْأَرْضِ أَنتَ وَلِيِّ فِى ٱلدُّنْيَا وَٱلْآخِرَةِ تَوَفَّنِى مُسْلِمًا وَأَلْحِقْنِى بِٱلصَّـٰلِحِينَ ۝

(يوسف ١٢:١٠١)

... رَبِّ ٱجْعَلْ هَـٰذَا ٱلْبَلَدَ ءَامِنًا وَٱجْنُبْنِى وَبَنِىَّ أَن نَّعْبُدَ ٱلْأَصْنَامَ ۝ رَبِّ إِنَّهُنَّ أَضْلَلْنَ كَثِيرًا مِّنَ ٱلنَّاسِ فَمَن تَبِعَنِى فَإِنَّهُۥ مِنِّى وَمَنْ عَصَانِى فَإِنَّكَ غَفُورٌ رَّحِيمٌ ۝ رَّبَّنَا إِنِّىۤ أَسْكَنتُ مِن ذُرِّيَّتِى بِوَادٍ غَيْرِ ذِى زَرْعٍ عِندَ بَيْتِكَ ٱلْمُحَرَّمِ رَبَّنَا لِيُقِيمُوا۟ ٱلصَّلَوٰةَ فَٱجْعَلْ أَفْـِٔدَةً مِّنَ ٱلنَّاسِ تَهْوِىٓ إِلَيْهِمْ وَٱرْزُقْهُم مِّنَ ٱلثَّمَرَٰتِ لَعَلَّهُمْ يَشْكُرُونَ ۝

(ابراهيم ١٤:٣٥-٣٧)

**DAY 39**

*O*ur Lord, You know what we conceal and what we reveal, and nothing is hidden from Allah on earth or in the heavens.

(Ibrahim 14:38)

**DAY 40**

*O* my Lord, make me and my offspring regular in prayer. O our Lord, accept our prayers.

(Ibrahim 14:40)

رَبَّنَآ إِنَّكَ تَعْلَمُ مَا نُخْفِي وَمَا نُعْلِنُ ۗ وَمَا يَخْفَىٰ عَلَى ٱللَّهِ مِن شَىْءٍ فِى ٱلْأَرْضِ وَلَا فِى ٱلسَّمَآءِ ۞

(ابراهيم ١٤: ٣٨)

رَبِّ ٱجْعَلْنِي مُقِيمَ ٱلصَّلَوٰةِ وَمِن ذُرِّيَّتِي ۚ رَبَّنَا وَتَقَبَّلْ دُعَآءِ ۞

(ابراهيم ١٤: ٤٠)

**DAY**
**41**

*O*ur Lord, forgive me, my parents and the believers on the Day of Judgement.

(Ibrahim 14:41)

**DAY**
**42**

*O* my Lord, have mercy on them [my parents] as they brought me up when I was small.

(al-Isra' 17:24)

اليوم
٤١

رَبَّنَا ٱغْفِرْ لِى وَلِوَالِدَىَّ وَلِلْمُؤْمِنِينَ يَوْمَ يَقُومُ ٱلْحِسَابُ ۝

(ابراهيم ١٤:٤١)

اليوم
٤٢

... رَبِّ ٱرْحَمْهُمَا كَمَا رَبَّيَانِى صَغِيرًا ۝

(الإسراء ١٧:٢٤)

**DAY 43**

*O* my Lord, let my entry be by the gate of truth
and my exit be by the gate of truth, and
support me with authority from Yourself.

(al-Isra' 17:80)

**DAY 44**

*G* ive me a heir out of Your grace. He should be
my heir and the heir of the family of Jacob,
and, O my Lord, make him pleasing to You.

(Maryam 19:5-6)

... رَّبِّ أَدْخِلْنِي مُدْخَلَ صِدْقٍ وَأَخْرِجْنِي مُخْرَجَ صِدْقٍ وَٱجْعَل لِّي مِن لَّدُنكَ سُلْطَٰنًا نَّصِيرًا ۝

(الإسراء ١٧: ٨٠)

... فَهَبْ لِي مِن لَّدُنكَ وَلِيًّا ۝ يَرِثُنِي وَيَرِثُ مِنْ ءَالِ يَعْقُوبَ ۖ وَٱجْعَلْهُ رَبِّ رَضِيًّا ۝

(مريم ١٩: ٥-٦)

*O* my Lord, open my breast for me, and make my task easy for me. Remove the impediment from my speech so that people may understand what I say.

(Ta' Ha' 20:25-28)

*O* my Lord, increase me in knowledge.

(Ta' Ha' 20:114)

اليوم
٤٥

رَبِّ ٱشْرَحْ لِى صَدْرِى ۝ وَيَسِّرْ لِىٓ أَمْرِى ۝ وَٱحْلُلْ
عُقْدَةً مِّن لِّسَانِى ۝ يَفْقَهُواْ قَوْلِى ۝

(طه ٢٠: ٢٥-٢٨)

اليوم
٤٦

رَّبِّ زِدْنِى عِلْمًا ۝

(طه ٢٠: ١١٤)

DAY
**47**

A disease has touched me and You are Most Merciful of those who show mercy.

(al-Anbiya' 21:83)

DAY
**48**

There is no god besides You [O Allah]. Glory be to You! Truly I have done wrong.

(al-Anbiya' 21:87)

...أَنِّي مَسَّنِيَ ٱلضُّرُّ وَأَنتَ أَرْحَمُ ٱلرَّاحِمِينَ ۝

(الأنبياء ٢١:٨٣)

...أَن لَّا إِلَٰهَ إِلَّا أَنتَ سُبْحَٰنَكَ إِنِّي كُنتُ
مِنَ ٱلظَّٰلِمِينَ ۝

(الأنبياء ٢١:٨٧)

*O* my Lord, do not leave me childless. You are the
Best of Inheritors.

(al-Anbiya' 21:89)

*O* my Lord, help me. They have called me a liar.

(al-Mu'minun 23:26)

اليوم
٤٩

... رَبِّ لَا تَذَرْنِي فَرْدًا وَأَنتَ خَيْرُ ٱلْوَٰرِثِينَ ۝

(الأنبياء ٢١:٨٩)

اليوم
٥٠

... رَبِّ ٱنصُرْنِي بِمَا كَذَّبُونِ ۝

(المؤمنون ٢٣:٢٦)

DAY
51

*O* my Lord, bless my landing. You are the best of those to make me land safely.

(al-Mu'minun 23:29)

DAY
52

*O* my Lord, if you show me the punishment which they were warned of in my presence, then, O my Lord, do not include me among the wrongdoers.

(al-Mu'minun 23:93-94)

اليوم
٥١

... رَّبِّ أَنزِلْنِي مُنزَلًا مُّبَارَكًا وَأَنتَ خَيْرُ ٱلْمُنزِلِينَ ۝

(المؤمنون ٢٣: ٢٩)

اليوم
٥٢

... رَّبِّ إِمَّا تُرِيَنِّي مَا يُوعَدُونَ ۝ رَبِّ فَلَا تَجْعَلْنِي فِي ٱلْقَوْمِ ٱلظَّـٰلِمِينَ ۝

(المؤمنون ٢٣: ٩٣-٩٤)

O my Lord, I take Your protection against the suggestions of the evil ones. O my Lord, I seek refuge in You should they approach me.

(al-Mu'minun 23:97-98)

O our Lord, we have accepted faith, so forgive us and have mercy on us for You are the best of those who show mercy.

(al-Mu'minun 23:109)

... رَبِّ أَعُوذُ بِكَ مِنْ هَمَزَاتِ ٱلشَّيَطِينِ ۞ وَأَعُوذُ بِكَ رَبِّ أَن يَحْضُرُونِ ۞

(المؤمنون ٢٣: ٩٧-٩٨)

... رَبَّنَآ ءَامَنَّا فَٱغْفِرْ لَنَا وَٱرْحَمْنَا وَأَنتَ خَيْرُ ٱلرَّٰحِمِينَ ۞

(المؤمنون ٢٣: ١٠٩)

*O* my Lord, forgive and have mercy for You are the best of those who show mercy.

(al-Mu'minun 23:118)

*O* my Lord, keep the punishment of Hell away from us, for its chastisement is binding. It is indeed a terrible abode and an evil resting place.

(al-Furqan 25:65-66)

... رَبِّ ٱغۡفِرۡ وَٱرۡحَمۡ وَأَنتَ خَيۡرُ ٱلرَّٰحِمِينَ ۝

(المؤمنون ٢٣: ١١٨)

... رَّبَّنَا ٱصۡرِفۡ عَنَّا عَذَابَ جَهَنَّمَ إِنَّ عَذَابَهَا كَانَ غَرَامًا ۝ إِنَّهَا سَآءَتۡ مُسۡتَقَرًّا وَمُقَامًا ۝

(الفرقان ٢٥: ٦٥-٦٦)

O my Lord, grant us such wives and children who will be a joy to our eyes, and make us leaders of the pious.

(al-Furqan 25:74)

O my Lord, grant me wisdom and join me with the pious, give me a good reputation among future generations, and make me deserving of the Garden of Bliss, and forgive my father, for he is among those who have strayed. And do not humiliate me on the Day of Judgement when all will be brought back to life, on the Day when neither one's children nor wealth will help, but only he who brings to Allah a sound heart [will be successful].

(al-Shu'ara' 26:83-89)

... رَبَّنَا هَبْ لَنَا مِنْ أَزْوَاجِنَا وَذُرِّيَّتِنَا قُرَّةَ أَعْيُنٍ وَٱجْعَلْنَا لِلْمُتَّقِينَ إِمَامًا ۝

(الفرقان ٢٥: ٧٤)

اليوم
٥٨

رَبِّ هَبْ لِى حُكْمًا وَأَلْحِقْنِى بِٱلصَّـٰلِحِينَ ۝ وَٱجْعَل لِّى لِسَانَ صِدْقٍ فِى ٱلْءَاخِرِينَ ۝ وَٱجْعَلْنِى مِن وَرَثَةِ جَنَّةِ ٱلنَّعِيمِ ۝ وَٱغْفِرْ لِأَبِىٓ إِنَّهُۥ كَانَ مِنَ ٱلضَّآلِّينَ ۝ وَلَا تُخْزِنِى يَوْمَ يُبْعَثُونَ ۝ يَوْمَ لَا يَنفَعُ مَالٌ وَلَا بَنُونَ ۝ إِلَّا مَنْ أَتَى ٱللَّهَ بِقَلْبٍ سَلِيمٍ ۝

(الشعراء ٢٦: ٨٣-٨٩)

**DAY 59**

*O* my Lord, my people have rejected me, so make a clear judgement between me and them, and grant deliverance to me and the believers who are with me.

(al-Shu'ara' 26:117-118)

**DAY 60**

*O* my Lord, grant deliverance to me and my family from [the evil consequences of] what they do.

(al-Shu'ara' 26:169)

...رَبِّ إِنَّ قَوْمِي كَذَّبُونِ ۝ فَافْتَحْ بَيْنِي وَبَيْنَهُمْ فَتْحًا وَنَجِّنِي
وَمَن مَّعِيَ مِنَ ٱلْمُؤْمِنِينَ ۝

(الشعراء ٢٦: ١١٧-١١٨)

رَبِّ نَجِّنِي وَأَهْلِي مِمَّا يَعْمَلُونَ ۝

(الشعراء ٢٦: ١٦٩)

**DAY 61**

O my Lord, enable me to thank You for the favours You have granted me and my parents. Let me do such good acts which may please You. By Your grace include me among Your pious servants.

(al-Naml 27:19)

**DAY 62**

O my Lord, I have wronged myself. Now, with Solomon, I submit myself to Allah, the Lord of the universe.

(al-Naml 27:44)

**اليوم ٦١**

... رَبِّ أَوْزِعْنِي أَنْ أَشْكُرَ نِعْمَتَكَ ٱلَّتِي أَنْعَمْتَ عَلَيَّ وَعَلَىٰ وَالِدَيَّ وَأَنْ أَعْمَلَ صَالِحًا تَرْضَاهُ وَأَدْخِلْنِي بِرَحْمَتِكَ فِي عِبَادِكَ ٱلصَّالِحِينَ ۝

(النمل ٢٧: ١٩)

**اليوم ٦٢**

... رَبِّ إِنِّي ظَلَمْتُ نَفْسِي وَأَسْلَمْتُ مَعَ سُلَيْمَانَ لِلَّهِ رَبِّ ٱلْعَالَمِينَ ۝

(النمل ٢٧: ٤٤)

**DAY 63**

*O* my Lord, I have wronged myself, so forgive me.

(al-Qasas 28:16)

**DAY 64**

*O* my Lord, as You have favoured me, I will never support the guilty.

(al-Qasas 28:17)

اليوم
٦٣

… رَبِّ إِنِّى ظَلَمْتُ نَفْسِى فَٱغْفِرْ لِى … ۝

(القصص ٢٨:١٦)

اليوم
٦٤

… رَبِّ بِمَآ أَنْعَمْتَ عَلَىَّ فَلَنْ أَكُونَ ظَهِيرًا لِّلْمُجْرِمِينَ ۝

(القصص ٢٨:١٧)

**DAY 65**

*O* my Lord, deliver me from the wrongdoers.

(al-Qasas 28:21)

**DAY 66**

*O* my Lord, I am really in need of any good that You may send me.

(al-Qasas 28:24)

... رَبِّ نَجِّنِي مِنَ ٱلْقَوْمِ ٱلظَّـٰلِمِينَ ۞

(القصص ٢٨: ٢١)

... رَبِّ إِنِّي لِمَآ أَنزَلْتَ إِلَىَّ مِنْ خَيْرٍ فَقِيرٌ ۞

(القصص ٢٨: ٢٤)

DAY
**67**

*O* my Lord, help me against the mischief-makers.

(al-'Ankabut 29:30)

DAY
**68**

*O* my Lord, grant me a pious son.

(al-Saffat 37:100)

اليوم
٦٧

۞ ...رَبِّ ٱنصُرۡنِي عَلَى ٱلۡقَوۡمِ ٱلۡمُفۡسِدِينَ

(العنكبوت ٢٩:٣٠)

اليوم
٦٨

۞ رَبِّ هَبۡ لِي مِنَ ٱلصَّـٰلِحِينَ

(الصافات ٣٧:١٠٠)

O our Lord, Your mercy and knowledge encompass everything. So forgive those who repent and follow Your way, and save them from the punishment of the Hellfire. O our Lord, admit them to the everlasting Gardens [of Paradise] You have promised them, and their pious fathers, wives and children. Surely You alone are Almighty, the Wisest; and guard them from all ills. He who is guarded by You against ills on the Day of Judgement, on him You have shown great mercy. That is the great triumph.

(al-Mu'min 40:7-9)

Glory be to Him Who subjected this [anything which is used for travel] to us, otherwise we could not have subdued it. To our Lord is our eventual return.

(al-Zukhruf 43:13-14)

... رَبَّنَا وَسِعْتَ كُلَّ شَيْءٍ رَّحْمَةً وَعِلْمًا فَاغْفِرْ لِلَّذِينَ تَابُوا وَاتَّبَعُوا سَبِيلَكَ وَقِهِمْ عَذَابَ الْجَحِيمِ ۞ رَبَّنَا وَأَدْخِلْهُمْ جَنَّاتِ عَدْنٍ الَّتِي وَعَدْتَّهُمْ وَمَن صَلَحَ مِنْ ءَابَآئِهِمْ وَأَزْوَٰجِهِمْ وَذُرِّيَّٰتِهِمْ إِنَّكَ أَنتَ الْعَزِيزُ الْحَكِيمُ ۞ وَقِهِمُ السَّيِّئَاتِ وَمَن تَقِ السَّيِّئَاتِ يَوْمَئِذٍ فَقَدْ رَحِمْتَهُ وَذَٰلِكَ هُوَ الْفَوْزُ الْعَظِيمُ ۞

(المؤمن ٤٠: ٧-٩)

... سُبْحَٰنَ الَّذِي سَخَّرَ لَنَا هَٰذَا وَمَا كُنَّا لَهُ مُقْرِنِينَ ۞ وَإِنَّآ إِلَىٰ رَبِّنَا لَمُنقَلِبُونَ ۞

(الزخرف ٤٣: ١٣-١٤)

**DAY**
**71**

O my Lord, enable me to thank You for Your favours which You did to me and my parents, enable me to keep doing good deeds which would please You, and make my offspring pious. I repent to You, and I am among those who surrender themselves to You.

(al-Ahqaf 46:15)

**DAY**
**72**

O our Lord, forgive us and our brothers who accepted faith before us, and do not leave in our hearts any ill-feeling towards other believers. O our Lord, You are the Kindest, Most Merciful.

(al-Hashr 59:10)

... رَبِّ أَوْزِعْنِي أَنْ أَشْكُرَ نِعْمَتَكَ ٱلَّتِي أَنْعَمْتَ عَلَيَّ وَعَلَىٰ
وَالِدَيَّ وَأَنْ أَعْمَلَ صَالِحًا تَرْضَاهُ وَأَصْلِحْ لِي فِي ذُرِّيَّتِيٓ
إِنِّي تُبْتُ إِلَيْكَ وَإِنِّي مِنَ ٱلْمُسْلِمِينَ ﴿١٥﴾

(الأحقاف ٤٦: ١٥)

... رَبَّنَا ٱغْفِرْ لَنَا وَلِإِخْوَانِنَا ٱلَّذِينَ سَبَقُونَا بِٱلْإِيمَانِ
وَلَا تَجْعَلْ فِي قُلُوبِنَا غِلًّا لِّلَّذِينَ ءَامَنُوا۟ رَبَّنَآ إِنَّكَ
رَءُوفٌ رَّحِيمٌ ﴿١٠﴾

(الحشر ٥٩: ١٠)

**DAY 73**

O our Lord, we put our trust in You, and to You we have turned, and to You is our eventual return. O our Lord, do not make us a test for the unbelievers, and forgive us, our Lord. You are Almighty, the Wisest.

(al-Mumtahinah 60:4-5)

**DAY 74**

O our Lord, perfect our light for us and forgive us. Truly You have power over everything.

(al-Tahrim 66:8)

... رَبَّنَا عَلَيْكَ تَوَكَّلْنَا وَإِلَيْكَ أَنَبْنَا وَإِلَيْكَ ٱلْمَصِيرُ ۝ رَبَّنَا لَا تَجْعَلْنَا فِتْنَةً لِّلَّذِينَ كَفَرُواْ وَٱغْفِرْ لَنَا رَبَّنَآ إِنَّكَ أَنتَ ٱلْعَزِيزُ ٱلْحَكِيمُ ۝

(الممتحنة ٦٠: ٤-٥)

... رَبَّنَآ أَتْمِمْ لَنَا نُورَنَا وَٱغْفِرْ لَنَآ إِنَّكَ عَلَىٰ كُلِّ شَىْءٍ قَدِيرٌ ۝

(التحريم ٦٦: ٨)

O my Lord, build for me a house near You in Paradise, and deliver me from Pharaoh and his evil deeds, and from the evildoers.

(al-Tahrim 66:11)

O my Lord, forgive me, my parents and everyone who enters my house as a believer, and forgive all believing men and women, and do not increase the wrongdoers in anything but their loss and destruction.

(al-Nuh 71:28)

اليوم
٧٥

رَبِّ ٱبْنِ لِى عِندَكَ بَيْتًا فِى ٱلْجَنَّةِ وَنَجِّنِى مِن فِرْعَوْنَ
وَعَمَلِهِۦ وَنَجِّنِى مِنَ ٱلْقَوْمِ ٱلظَّـٰلِمِينَ ۝

(التحريم ٦٦:١١)

اليوم
٧٦

رَّبِّ ٱغْفِرْ لِى وَلِوَٰلِدَىَّ وَلِمَن دَخَلَ بَيْتِىَ مُؤْمِنًا وَلِلْمُؤْمِنِينَ
وَٱلْمُؤْمِنَـٰتِ وَلَا تَزِدِ ٱلظَّـٰلِمِينَ إِلَّا تَبَارًا ۝

(نوح ٧١: ٢٨)

DAY
**77**

Say: I seek safety and protection with the Lord of the rising day; from the evil of all that which he has created; from the evil of the night when the darkness spreads; from the evil of women when they blow on knots; and from the envier when he envies.

(al-Falaq 113:1-5)

DAY
**78**

Say: I seek safety and protection with the Lord of all people, the King of all people, and the God of all people from the evil of the whisperer, who whispers into the hearts of people, whether they are Jinn or people.

(al-Nas 114:1-6)

قُلْ أَعُوذُ بِرَبِّ ٱلْفَلَقِ ۞ مِن شَرِّ مَا خَلَقَ ۞ وَمِن شَرِّ
غَاسِقٍ إِذَا وَقَبَ ۞ وَمِن شَرِّ ٱلنَّفَّـٰثَـٰتِ فِى ٱلْعُقَدِ ۞ وَمِن
شَرِّ حَاسِدٍ إِذَا حَسَدَ ۞

(الفلق ١١٣: ١-٥)

قُلْ أَعُوذُ بِرَبِّ ٱلنَّاسِ ۞ مَلِكِ ٱلنَّاسِ ۞ إِلَـٰهِ ٱلنَّاسِ ۞
مِن شَرِّ ٱلْوَسْوَاسِ ٱلْخَنَّاسِ ۞ ٱلَّذِى يُوَسْوِسُ فِى صُدُورِ
ٱلنَّاسِ ۞ مِنَ ٱلْجِنَّةِ وَٱلنَّاسِ ۞

(الناس ١١٤: ١-٦)

# Daily Wisdom

*Prophetic Prayers &*
*Supplications*

### On getting up

Praise be to Allah who has brought us back to life after causing our death and to Him is the resurrection.

(B/M)

### After dawn

There is no god except Allah alone, Who has no partner. To Him belongs the kingdom and all praise and He has power over all things.

(AD)

اليوم
٧٩

**عند الإستيقاظ من النوم**

الْحَمْدُ لِلَّهِ الَّذِى أَحْيَانَا بَعْدَ مَا أَمَاتَنَا وَإِلَيْهِ النُّشُورُ

البخاري : كتاب الدعوات/ ٦٣١٢ ، مسلم : كتاب الذكر والدعاء/ ٢٧١١

اليوم
٨٠

**بعد الفجر**

لَا إِلَهَ إِلَّا اللهُ وَحْدَهُ ، لَا شَرِيكَ لَهُ ، لَهُ الْمُلْكُ ، وَلَهُ الْحَمْدُ ، وَهُوَ عَلَى كُلِّ شَيْءٍ قَدِيرٌ

أبو داوود : كتاب الأدب/ ٥٠٧٧

### DAY 81

Praise be to Allah Who has forgiven us on this day and did not destroy us because of our sins.

(M)

### DAY 82

Praise be to Allah Who has gifted us this day, forgave us the slips we committed throughout it and did not chastise us with the Fire.

(T)

عند الشروق:

اَلْحَمْدُ لِلَّهِ الَّذِى أَقَالَنَا يَوْمَنَا هَذَا وَلَمْ يُهْلِكْنَا بِذُنُوبِنَا

مسلم : كتاب صلاة المسافرين/ ٨٢٢

عند الشروق:

الْحَمْدُ لِلَّهِ الَّذِى وَهَبَ لَنَا هَذَا الْيَوْمَ، وَأَقَالَنَا فِيهِ عَثَرَاتِنَا
وَلَمْ يُعَذِّبْنَا بِالنَّارِ

الكبير للطبراني : جزء ٩/ رقم الحديث : ٨٩٠١

### DAY 83

#### IN THE MORNINGS

(O Lord,) we have reached the morning while following the primordial nature of Islam, the testimony of oneness, the religion of our Prophet Muhammad and the way of our father Ibrahim, who was upright and surrendered to Allah, and I am not of those who associate partners with Allah.

(IS/A)

### DAY 84

#### IN THE MORNINGS

We have reached the morning and the dominion belongs to Allah, Mighty and Majestic is He; praise, grandeur, might, creation and command all belong to Allah; the night and day as well as what lies still in them also belong to Allah, Mighty and Majestic is He. O Allah, make this day begin with righteousness, crown its middle part with success and conclude its end with prosperity, O Most Merciful among those who possess mercy.

(IS)

**اليوم ٨٣**

## في الصباح

أَصْبَحْنَا عَلَى فِطْرَةِ الإِسْلَامِ، وَكَلِمَةِ الإِخْلَاصِ، وَدِينِ نَبِيِّنَا مُحَمَّدٍ، وَمِلَّةِ أَبِينَا إِبْرَاهِيمَ حَنِيفًا مُسْلِمًا، وَمَا أَنَا مِنَ الْمُشْرِكِينَ

ابن السني : رقم الحديث ٣٤ ، أحمد : رقم الحديث ١٥٣٦٠

**اليوم ٨٤**

## في الصباح

أَصْبَحْنَا وَأَصْبَحَ الْمُلْكُ لِلَّهِ عَزَّ وَجَلَّ ، وَالْحَمْدُ لِلَّهِ ، وَالْكِبْرِيَاءُ وَالْعَظَمَةُ لِلَّهِ ، وَالْخَلْقُ وَالْأَمْرُ ، وَاللَّيْلُ وَالنَّهَارُ وَمَا سَكَنَ فِيهِمَا لِلَّهِ عَزَّ وَجَلَّ ، اللَّهُمَّ اجْعَلْ أَوَّلَ هَذَا النَّهَارِ صَلَاحًا ، وَأَوْسَطَهُ نَجَاحًا ، وَآخِرَهُ فَلَاحًا ، يَا أَرْحَمَ الرَّاحِمِينَ

ابن السني : رقم الحديث ٣٨

### DAY 85

Allah, it is through You that we have lived to this morning and it is through You that we will live until the evening; it is through You that we live and it is through You that we die, and unto You is the return.

(T/AD)

### DAY 86

Allah, any blessing that I or anyone else of Your creation possess this morning is from You alone, You have no partners, so all praise and all thanks are due to You.

(AD)

اليوم
٨٥

في الصباح

اللَّهُمَّ بِكَ أَصْبَحْنَا وَبِكَ أَمْسَيْنَا وَبِكَ نَحْيَا وَبِكَ نَمُوتُ
وَإِلَيْكَ النُّشُورُ

الترمذي : كتاب الدعوات/ ٣٣٩١، أبو داوود : كتاب الأدب/ ٥٠٦٨

اليوم
٨٦

في الصباح

اللَّهُمَّ مَا أَصْبَحَ بِي مِنْ نِعْمَةٍ، أَوْ بِأَحَدٍ مِنْ خَلْقِكَ، فَمِنْكَ
وَحْدَكَ لاَ شَرِيكَ لَكَ، فَلَكَ الْحَمْدُ وَلَكَ الشُّكْرُ

أبو داوود : كتاب الأدب/ ٥٠٧٣

### IN THE MORNINGS AND EVENINGS

O Allah, You are my Lord; there is no god besides You; I am Your slave; and You have created me. I will hold true to Your promise and pledge as much as is in my power; I seek refuge in You from the evil I have created; I acknowledge Your blessings on me and I admit my sins; so forgive me, for none forgives sins except You.

(B/T)

### IN THE MORNINGS AND EVENINGS

We have lived to see the evening and the dominion belongs to Allah. Praise be to Allah; there is no god except Allah, alone without any partners; to Him belongs the dominion and praise and He has power over all things. O Lord, I ask You for the good that is in this night and for the good that is in what comes after it, and I seek refuge in You from the evil

في الصباح والمساء

اللَّهُمَّ أَنْتَ رَبِّي لَا إِلَهَ إِلَّا أَنْتَ خَلَقْتَنِي وَأَنَا عَبْدُكَ وَأَنَا عَلَى عَهْدِكَ وَوَعْدِكَ مَا اسْتَطَعْتُ أَعُوذُ بِكَ مِنْ شَرِّ مَا صَنَعْتُ أَبُوءُ لَكَ بِنِعْمَتِكَ عَلَيَّ وَأَبُوءُ لَكَ بِذَنْبِي فَاغْفِرْ لِي فَإِنَّهُ لَا يَغْفِرُ الذُّنُوبَ إِلَّا أَنْتَ

البخاري: كتاب الدعوات/ ٦٣٠٦، الترمذي: كتاب الدعوات/ ٣٣٩٣

في الصباح والمساء

أَمْسَيْنَا وَأَمْسَى الْمُلْكُ لِلَّهِ، وَالْحَمْدُ لِلَّهِ، لَا إِلَهَ إِلَّا اللَّهُ، وَحْدَهُ لَا شَرِيكَ لَهُ، لَهُ الْمُلْكُ وَلَهُ الْحَمْدُ وَهُوَ عَلَى كُلِّ شَيْءٍ قَدِيرٌ، رَبِّ أَسْأَلُكَ خَيْرَ مَا فِي هَذِهِ اللَّيْلَةِ وَخَيْرَ مَا بَعْدَهَا، وَأَعُوذُ بِكَ مِنْ شَرِّ مَا فِي هَذِهِ اللَّيْلَةِ وَشَرِّ

of this night and the evil that is in what comes after it. O Lord I seek refuge in You from laziness and decrepitude. O Lord I seek refuge in You from the chastisement of Hellfire and the chastisement of the grave.

(M)

## DAY
## 89

In the name of Allah with Whose name nothing harms [one] on the earth or in the sky [heaven] and He is the All-Hearing, All-Knowing.

(AD/T)

مَا بَعْدَهَا، رَبِّ أَعُوذُ بِكَ مِنَ الْكَسَلِ وَسُوءِ الْكِبَرِ،
رَبِّ أَعُوذُ بِكَ مِنْ عَذَابٍ فِي النَّارِ وَعَذَابٍ فِي الْقَبْرِ

مسلم: كتاب الذكر والدعاء/ رقم الحديث ٢٧٢٣

**اليوم**
**٨٩**

## في الصباح والمساء

بِسْمِ اللهِ الَّذِى لاَ يَضُرُّ مَعَ اسْمِهِ شَىْءٌ فِى الْأَرْضِ وَلاَ فِى
السَّمَاءِ وَهُوَ السَّمِيعُ الْعَلِيمُ

أبو داوود: كتاب الأدب/ ٥٠٨٨ ، الترمذي: كتاب الدعوات/ ٣٣٨٨

## DAY 90

O Allah, grant me well-being to my body and my hearing. O Allah, grant me well-being in my sight; there is no god besides You.

(AD/A)

## DAY 91

I am pleased with taking Allah as [my] Lord, Islam as [my] religion and Muhammad as [my] Prophet.

(T/AD)

في الصباح والمساء

اللَّهُمَّ عَافِنِي فِي بَدَنِي، اللَّهُمَّ عَافِنِي فِي سَمْعِي، اللَّهُمَّ عَافِنِي فِي بَصَرِي، لَا إِلَهَ إِلَّا أَنْتَ

أبو داوود : كتاب الأدب/ ٥٠٩٠ ، أحمد : رقم الحديث ٢٠٤٤٦

في الصباح والمساء

رَضِيْتُ بِاللَّهِ رَبًّا وَبِالْإِسْلَامِ دِيْنًا وَبِمُحَمَّدٍ نَبِيًّا

الترمذي : كتاب الدعوات/ ٣٣٨٩ ، أبو داوود : كتاب الأدب/ ٥٠٧٢

### IN THE MORNINGS AND EVENINGS

O Allah, I seek refuge in you from anxiety and grief, from impotence and lassitude, from cowardice and stinginess and from the burden of debt and being overpowered by men.

(B)

### IN THE MORNINGS AND EVENINGS

O Allah, I ask You well-being in this world and in the next; O Allah, I ask Your pardon and safety in my religion, worldly affairs, my family and property. O Allah, conceal my faults and protect me from the things I fear. And protect me from my front, from my rear, from my right, from my left, and from above me. And I seek refuge in Your greatness that I do not get destroyed by what is beneath me.

(AD)

في الصباح والمساء

اللَّهُمَّ إِنِّي أَعُوذُ بِكَ مِنَ الْهَمِّ وَالْحَزَنِ، وَالْعَجْزِ وَالْكَسَلِ،
وَالْجُبْنِ وَالْبُخْلِ، وَضَلَعِ الدَّيْنِ، وَغَلَبَةِ الرِّجَالِ

البخاري : كتاب الدعوات/ ٦٣٦٩

في الصباح والمساء

اللَّهُمَّ إِنِّي أَسْأَلُكَ الْعَافِيَةَ فِي الدُّنْيَا وَالْآخِرَةِ اللَّهُمَّ إِنِّي
أَسْأَلُكَ الْعَفْوَ وَالْعَافِيَةَ فِي دِينِي وَدُنْيَايَ وَأَهْلِي وَمَالِي اللَّهُمَّ
اسْتُرْ عَوْرَاتِي وَآمِنْ رَوْعَاتِي وَاحْفَظْنِي مِنْ بَيْنِ يَدَيَّ
وَمِنْ خَلْفِي وَعَنْ يَمِينِي وَعَنْ شِمَالِي وَمِنْ فَوْقِي وَأَعُوذُ
بِعَظَمَتِكَ أَنْ أُغْتَالَ مِنْ تَحْتِي

أبو داوود : كتاب الأدب/ ٥٠٧٤

**DAY**
**94**

My Lord is Allah, there is no god except Him, He is the Most High, the Mighty. I put my trust in Allah, and He is the Lord of the Mighty Throne. What Allah wills takes place, and what Allah does not will does not take place. I know that Allah has power over all things and that He encompasses all things with His knowledge.

(IS)

**DAY**
**95**

Glory be to Allah and all praise belongs to Him, there is no power except through Allah; what He wills takes place and what He does not will does not; I know that Allah has power over all things and that He encompasses all things with His knowledge.

(AD)

في الصباح والمساء

رَبِّيَ اللَّهُ الَّذِي لَا إِلَهَ إِلَّا هُوَ الْعَلِيُّ الْعَظِيمُ، تَوَكَّلْتُ عَلَى

اللَّهِ، وَهُوَ رَبُّ الْعَرْشِ الْعَظِيمِ، مَا شَاءَ اللَّهُ كَانَ، وَمَا لَمْ

يَشَأْ لَمْ يَكُنْ، أَعْلَمُ أَنَّ اللَّهَ عَلَى كُلِّ شَيْءٍ قَدِيرٌ، وَأَنَّ اللَّهَ قَدْ

أَحَاطَ بِكُلِّ شَيْءٍ عِلْمًا

ابن السني : رقم الحديث ٤٢

في الصباح والمساء

سُبْحَانَ اللَّهِ وَبِحَمْدِهِ لَا قُوَّةَ إِلَّا بِاللَّهِ مَا شَاءَ اللَّهُ كَانَ

وَمَا لَمْ يَشَأْ لَمْ يَكُنْ أَعْلَمُ أَنَّ اللَّهَ عَلَى كُلِّ شَيْءٍ قَدِيرٌ وَأَنَّ اللَّهَ

قَدْ أَحَاطَ بِكُلِّ شَيْءٍ عِلْمًا

أبو داوود : كتاب الأدب/ ٥٠٧٥

### DAY 96

**IN THE MORNINGS AND EVENINGS**

O Allah, I ask You of sudden goodness and seek refuge in you from sudden evil.

(IS)

### DAY 97

**IN THE MORNINGS AND EVENINGS**

O Ever-Living, O Self-Subsisting, I seek help in Your mercy; correct all my affairs and do not leave me to my ego, even for a glance of an eye.

(IS)

في الـصبـاح والـمسـاء

اَللّهُمَّ إِنِّي أَسْأَلُكَ مِنْ فَجْأَةِ الْخَيْرِ وَأَعُوذُ بِكَ مِنْ فَجْأَةِ الشَّرِّ

ابن السني : رقم الحديث ٣٩

في الـصبـاح والـمسـاء

يَا حَيُّ يَا قَيُّومُ بِرَحْمَتِكَ أَسْتَغِيثُ، أَصْلِحْ لِي شَأْنِي كُلَّهُ،
وَلَا تَكِلْنِي إِلَى نَفْسِي طَرْفَةَ عَيْنٍ

ابن السني : رقم الحديث ٤٨

## DAY 98

Allah is sufficient unto me, there is no god except Him, upon Him do I place my trust and He is the Lord of the Mighty Throne.

(AD)

## DAY 99

O Allah, You are the most deserving of being remembered, the most deserving of being worshipped, the most helpful when sought for help, the most tender among those who possess, the most generous among those who are asked, the One Who gives most among those who give. You are the Sovereign, You have no partner. You are the Unique Who perishes not; all things perish except Your Countenance. You will never be obeyed except through Your leave, and You have never been disobeyed except through Your Knowledge. You give

في الصباح والمساء

حَسْبِيَ اللهُ لاَ إِلَهَ إِلاَّ هُوَ عَلَيْهِ تَوَكَّلْتُ وَهُوَ رَبُّ الْعَرْشِ الْعَظِيمِ

أبو داوود : كتاب الأدب/ ٥٠٨١

في الصباح والمساء

اللّهُمَّ أَنْتَ أَحَقُّ مَنْ ذُكِرَ، وَأَحَقُّ مَنْ عُبِدَ، وَأَنْصَرُ مَنِ ابْتُغِيَ، وَأَرْأَفُ مَنْ مَلَكَ، وَأَجْوَدُ مَنْ سُئِلَ، وَأَوْسَعُ مَنْ أَعْطَى، أَنْتَ الْمَلِكُ لَا شَرِيكَ لَكَ، وَالْفَرْدُ لَا تَهْلِكُ، كُلُّ شَيْءٍ هَالِكٌ إِلَّا وَجْهَكَ لَنْ تُطَاعَ إِلَّا بِإِذْنِكَ، وَلَمْ تُعْصَ إِلَّا بِعِلْمِكَ، تُطَاعُ

thanks for being obeyed and You forgive when disobeyed. You are the closest Witness and the nearest Protector. You stand between one and the military garrisons of the enemies; You seize by the forelocks; You have preordained works and recorded the length of people's lifespans; hearts confess to You; and what is deemed secret is open to You. The lawful is that which You have made lawful, and the unlawful is that which You have made unlawful; religion is that which You have prescribed, and order is that which You have ordained. The creation is Your creation and the slave is Your slave and You are Allah, the Gracious, the Compassionate. I ask You by the light of Your Countenance by means of which the heavens and earth are illumined, and by every right due to You, as well as by the right of the beseechers upon You, to accept me in this morning (or evening) and to preserve me, by Your power, from Hellfire.

(TbD)

فَتَشْكُرُ، وَتُعْصَى فَتَغْفِرُ، أَقْرَبُ شَهِيدٍ وَأَدْنَى حَفِيظٍ، حُلْتَ دُونَ الثُّغُورِ، وَأَخَذْتَ بِالنَّوَاصِي، وَكَتَبْتَ الْأَثَارَ، وَنَسَخْتَ الْأَجَالَ الْقُلُوبُ لَكَ مُفْضِيَّةٌ وَالسِّرُّ عِنْدَكَ عَلَانِيَةٌ، الْحَلَالُ مَا أَحْلَلْتَ وَالْحَرَامُ مَا حَرَّمْتَ، وَالدِّينُ مَا شَرَعْتَ، وَالْأَمْرُ مَا قَضَيْتَ، وَالْخَلْقُ خَلْقُكَ، وَالْعَبْدُ عَبْدُكَ، وَأَنْتَ اللهُ الرَّءُوفُ الرَّحِيمُ، أَسْأَلُكَ بِنُورِ وَجْهِكَ الَّذِي أَشْرَقَتْ لَهُ السَّمَوَاتُ وَالْأَرْضُ، وَبِكُلِّ حَقٍّ هُوَ لَكَ، وَبِحَقِّ السَّائِلِينَ عَلَيْكَ، أَنْ تَقْبَلَنِي فِي هَذِهِ الْغَدَاةِ (أَوْ فِي هَذِهِ الْعَشِيَّةِ) وَأَنْ تُجِيرَنِي مِنَ النَّارِ بِقُدْرَتِكَ

الدعاء للطبراني : رقم الحديث ٣١٨

**DAY 100**

Allah, Creator of the heavens and earth, Knower of the unseen and the visible world, Lord and Master of all things, I bear witness that there is no god except You; I seek refuge in You from the evil of my self and from the evil and traps of the devil.

(AD)

**DAY 101**

IN THE MORNINGS AND EVENINGS

Allah, I have reached the morning (or evening) enjoying blessings, well-being and concealment [of my faults] from You, so prolong for me Your blessings, well-being and concealment [of my faults] in this world and in the next.

(IS)

**اليوم ١٠٠**

في الصباح والمساء

اللَّهُمَّ فَاطِرَ السَّمَوَاتِ وَالْأَرْضِ، عَالِمَ الْغَيْبِ وَالشَّهَادَةِ، رَبَّ كُلِّ شَيْءٍ وَمَلِيكَهُ، أَشْهَدُ أَنْ لَا إِلَهَ إِلَّا أَنْتَ، أَعُوذُ بِكَ مِنْ شَرِّ نَفْسِي، وَشَرِّ الشَّيْطَانِ وَشِرْكِهِ

أبو داوود: كتاب الأدب/ ٥٠٦٧

**اليوم ١٠١**

في الصباح والمساء

اللَّهُمَّ إِنِّي أَصْبَحْتُ (أَمْسَيْتُ) مِنْكَ فِي نِعْمَةٍ وَعَافِيَةٍ وَسِتْرٍ، فَأَتِمَّ عَلَيَّ نِعْمَتَكَ وَعَافِيَتَكَ وَسِتْرَكَ فِي الدُّنْيَا وَالْآخِرَةِ

ابن السني: رقم الحديث ٥٥

**DAY**
**102**

### IN THE EVENINGS

O Allah, I have reached the evening bearing witness to You and the carriers of Your Throne, the angels and all Your created beings affirming that You are Allah, there is no god except You and that Muhammad is Your slave and Messenger.

(AD)

**DAY**
**103**

### ON GOING TO BED

In Your name, O my Lord, I have put down my body [to rest] and it is through You that I will raise it; if You retain my soul, then please forgive it, but if You release it, then protect it with what You protect Your righteous slaves with.

(B)

### في المساء

اللَّهُمَّ إِنِّي أَمْسَيْتُ أُشْهِدُكَ وَأُشْهِدُ حَمَلَةَ عَرْشِكَ وَمَلاَئِكَتَكَ وَجَمِيعَ خَلْقِكَ أَنَّكَ أَنْتَ اللهُ لاَ إِلَهَ إِلاَّ أَنْتَ وَأَنَّ مُحَمَّدًا عَبْدُكَ وَرَسُولُكَ

أبو داوود: كتاب الأدب/ ٥٠٦٩

### عند الذهاب إلى النوم

بِاسْمِكَ رَبِّ وَضَعْتُ جَنْبِي وَبِكَ أَرْفَعُهُ، إِنْ أَمْسَكْتَ نَفْسِي فَاغْفِرْ لَهَا، وَإِنْ أَرْسَلْتَهَا فَاحْفَظْهَا بِمَا تَحْفَظُ بِهِ عِبَادَكَ الصَّالِحِينَ

البخاري: كتاب التوحيد/ ٧٣٩٣

### DAY
### 104

O Allah, I have surrendered my being to You, consigned my matter to You, and placed my body under Your care, out of desire for and awe of You; there is neither sanctuary nor escape from You except in You. O Allah, I have believed in the Book You have revealed and in Your Prophet whom You have sent.

(B)

### DAY
### 105

O Allah, I seek refuge in Your noble Countenance and in Your most perfect Words from the evil of those whom You have seized by the fore-locks. O Allah, it is You Who removes loss and sin. O Allah, Your army cannot be defeated, Your promise cannot be broken, the wealth of the wealthy cannot be of any avail to them; glory be to You and all praise belongs to You.

(AD)

### عند الذهاب إلى النوم

اللَّهُمَّ أَسْلَمْتُ وَجْهِي إِلَيْكَ، وَفَوَّضْتُ أَمْرِي إِلَيْكَ،
وَأَلْجَأْتُ ظَهْرِي إِلَيْكَ، رَغْبَةً وَرَهْبَةً إِلَيْكَ، لَا مَلْجَأَ
وَلَا مَنْجَا مِنْكَ إِلَّا إِلَيْكَ، اللَّهُمَّ ءَامَنْتُ بِكِتَابِكَ الَّذِي
أَنْزَلْتَ، وَبِنَبِيِّكَ الَّذِي أَرْسَلْتَ

البخاري: كتاب الوضوء/ ٢٤٧

### عند الذهاب إلى النوم

اللَّهُمَّ إِنِّي أَعُوذُ بِوَجْهِكَ الْكَرِيمِ وَكَلِمَاتِكَ التَّامَّةِ مِنْ
شَرِّ مَا أَنْتَ ءَاخِذٌ بِنَاصِيَتِهِ اللَّهُمَّ أَنْتَ تَكْشِفُ الْمَغْرَمَ وَالْمَأْثَمَ
اللَّهُمَّ لَا يُهْزَمُ جُنْدُكَ وَلَا يُخْلَفُ وَعْدُكَ وَلَا يَنْفَعُ ذَا الْجَدِّ
مِنْكَ الْجَدُّ سُبْحَانَكَ وَبِحَمْدِكَ

أبو داوود: كتاب الأدب/ ٥٠٥٢

### DAY 106

ON GOING TO BED

Praise be to Allah Who has granted me sufficiency and shelter, fed me and given me drink;
He has lavishly bestowed His blessings upon
me and given to me in abundance. Praise be to
Allah in all eventualities. O Allah, Lord, Master
and Sovereign of all things, I seek refuge in
You from the Fire.

(AD)

### DAY 107

BEFORE FALLING ASLEEP IN BED

O Allah, spare me Your punishment on the Day
when You will bring Your slaves back to life.

(AD/T)

### عند الذهاب إلى النوم

الْحَمْدُ للهِ الَّذِى كَفَانِى وَءَاوَانِى ، وَأَطْعَمَنِى وَسَقَانِى ، وَالَّذِى مَنَّ عَلَىَّ فَأَفْضَلَ ، وَالَّذِى أَعْطَانِى فَأَجْزَلَ ، الْحَمْدُ للهِ عَلَى كُلِّ حَالٍ اللَّهُمَّ رَبَّ كُلِّ شَىْءٍ وَمَلِيكَهُ وَإِلَهَ كُلِّ شَىْءٍ ، أَعُوذُ بِكَ مِنَ النَّارِ

أبو داوود : كتاب الأدب/ ٥٠٥٨

### عند النوم

اللَّهُمَّ قِنِى عَذَابَكَ يَوْمَ تَبْعَثُ عِبَادَكَ

أبو داوود : كتاب الأدب/ ٥٠٤٥ ، الترمذي : كتاب الدعوات/ ٣٣٩٨

## DAY 108

O Allah, in Your name I die and come back to life.

(B)

## DAY 109

O Allah, Lord of the seven heavens and all that they shade, and Lord of the earths and all they carry, and Lord of the devils and all those whom they lead astray, protect me from the evil of all your created beings, lest any one of them transgresses against me or oppresses me. He who is protected by You is mighty, Your praise is lofty, there is no other deity but You, and there is no god except You.

(T)

عند النوم

اللَّهُمَّ بِاسْمِكَ أَمُوتُ وَأَحْيَا

البخاري : كتاب الدعوات/ ٦٣١٤

عند الأرق

اللَّهُمَّ رَبَّ السَّمَوَاتِ السَّبْعِ وَمَا أَظَلَّتْ وَرَبَّ الأَرَضِينَ
وَمَا أَقَلَّتْ وَرَبَّ الشَّيَاطِينِ وَمَا أَضَلَّتْ كُنْ لِي جَارًا مِنْ
شَرِّ خَلْقِكَ كُلِّهِمْ جَمِيعًا أَنْ يَفْرُطَ عَلَيَّ أَحَدٌ مِنْهُمْ أَوْ أَنْ
يَبْغِيَ عَلَيَّ عَزَّ جَارُكَ وَجَلَّ ثَنَاؤُكَ وَلاَ إِلَهَ غَيْرُكَ، وَلاَ إِلَهَ
إِلاَّ أَنْتَ

الترمذي : كتاب الدعوات/ ٣٥٢٣

## DAY 110

### WHEN UNABLE TO SLEEP

O Allah, the stars have emerged, the eyes seek rest, and You are Ever-Living, Self-Subsisting. Neither slumber nor sleep overtakes You. O Ever-Living, O Self-Subsisting, grant me rest and put my eyes to sleep.

(IS)

## DAY 111

### AFTER A NIGHTMARE

I seek refuge in Allah's most perfect words from His anger, punishment, the evil of His servants and from the insinuations and promptings of the devils.

(AD/T)

**عند الأرق**

اللَّهُمَّ غَارَتِ النُّجُومُ، وَهَدَأَتِ الْعُيُونُ، وَأَنْتَ حَىٌّ قَيُّومُ،

لَا تَأْخُذُكَ سِنَةٌ وَلَا نَوْمٌ، يَا حَىٌّ يَا قَيُّومُ، أَهْدِئْ لَيْلِى،

وَأَنِمْ عَيْنِى

ابن السني : رقم الحديث ٧٤٩

**عند الفزع من النوم**

أَعُوذُ بِكَلِمَاتِ اللهِ التَّامَّةِ، مِنْ غَضَبِهِ وَعِقَابِهِ وَشَرِّ عِبَادِهِ

وَمِنْ هَمَزَاتِ الشَّيَاطِينِ وَأَنْ يَحْضُرُونِ

أبو داوود : كتاب الطب/ ٣٨٩٣، الترمذي : كتاب الدعوات/ ٣٥٢٨

### DAY 112

##### AFTER A NIGHTMARE

O Allah, I seek refuge in You from the work of the devil and bad dreams, for they will come to nothing.

(IS)

### DAY 113

##### ON GETTING UP AT NIGHT

There is no god except You, glory be to You. O Allah, I seek Your forgiveness of my sins and I ask for Your mercy. O Allah, increase my knowledge, do not allow my heart to deviate after You have guided me and grant me from Your presence mercy; verily You are the Best of those who give.

(AD/IS)

عند الفزع من النوم

اللَّهُمَّ إِنِّي أَعُوذُ بِكَ مِنْ عَمَلِ الشَّيْطَانِ، وَسَيِّئَاتِ الْأَحْلَامِ

ابن السني : رقم الحديث ٧٧٠

عند الاستيقاظ من الليل

لَا إِلَهَ إِلاَّ أَنْتَ سُبْحَانَكَ اللَّهُمَّ أَسْتَغْفِرُكَ لِذَنْبِي وَأَسْأَلُكَ رَحْمَتَكَ اللَّهُمَّ زِدْنِي عِلْمًا وَلاَ تُزِغْ قَلْبِي بَعْدَ إِذْ هَدَيْتَنِي وَهَبْ لِي مِنْ لَدُنْكَ رَحْمَةً إِنَّكَ أَنْتَ الْوَهَّابُ

أبو داوود : كتاب الأدب/ ٥٠٦١ ، ابن السني : رقم الحديث : ٧٥٦

## DAY 114

ON GETTING UP AT NIGHT

There is no god except Allah, the One, the All-Conquering, Lord of the heavens and earth and what is in-between, the Almighty, the Most Forgiving.

(IS)

## DAY 115

ON ENTERING THE TOILET

O Allah, I seek refuge in You from filth and from male and female jinns.

(B)

**اليوم ١١٤**

### عند الاستيقاظ من الليل

لَا إِلَهَ إِلَّا اللهُ الْوَاحِدُ الْقَهَّارُ، رَبُّ السَّمَوَاتِ وَالْأَرْضِ وَمَا بَيْنَهُمَا الْعَزِيزُ الْغَفَّارُ

ابن السني : رقم الحديث : ٧٥٧

**اليوم ١١٥**

### عند دخول الخلاء

اللَّهُمَّ إِنِّي أَعُوذُ بِكَ مِنَ الْخُبْثِ وَالْخَبَائِثِ

البخاري : كتاب الوضوء/ ١٤٢ ، مسلم : كتاب الحيض/ ٣٧٥

**DAY 116**

### On leaving the toilet

Praise be to Allah Who has removed harm from me and given me well-being.

(IS)

**DAY 117**

### On leaving the toilet

Praise be to Allah Who has allowed me to taste its pleasure [food], left in me its strength and removed from me its harm.

(IS)

عند الخروج من الخلاء

الْحَمْدُ لِلَّهِ الَّذِى أَذْهَبَ عَنِّى الْأَذَىٰ وَعَافَانِىْ

ابن السني : رقم الحديث ٢٢

عند الخروج من الخلاء

الْحَمْدُ لِلَّهِ الَّذِى أَذَاقَنِى لَذَّتَهُ، وَأَبْقَىٰ فِىَّ قُوَّتَهُ، وَأَذْهَبَ عَنِّى أَذَاهُ

ابن السني : رقم الحديث ٢٥

## DAY 118

### On leaving the toilet

 Allah,) I seek Your forgiveness.

(IS)

## DAY 119

### When completing ablution (wudu')

O Allah, forgive my sins, grant me abundance in my home and bless my sustenance for me.

(Tb)

**اليوم ١١٨**

عند الخروج من الخلاء

غُفْرَانَكَ

ابن السني : رقم الحديث ٢٣

**اليوم ١١٩**

بعد الوضوء

اللَّهُمَّ اغْفِرْ لِيْ ذَنْبِيْ، وَوَسِّعْ لِيْ فِيْ دَارِيْ، وَبَارِكْ لِيْ فِيْ رِزْقِيْ

الدعاء للطبراني : رقم الحديث ٦٥٦

**DAY**
**120**

###### WHEN COMPLETING ABLUTION (WUDU')

O Allah, make me among those who are oft-repentant and those who purify themselves.

(T)

**DAY**
**121**

###### WHEN COMPLETING ABLUTION (WUDU')

I bear witness that there is no god except Allah and that Muhammad is the slave and Messenger of Allah.

(M)

**اليوم ١٢٠**

بـعـد الـوضـوء

اللَّهُمَّ اجْعَلْنِي مِنَ التَّوَّابِينَ واجْعَلْنِي مِنَ الْمُتَطَهِّرِينَ

الترمذي : كتاب الطهارة/ رقم الحديث ٥٥

**اليوم ١٢١**

بـعـد الـوضـوء

أَشْهَدُ أَنْ لَا إِلَهَ إِلَّا اللهُ وَأَنَّ مُحَمَّدًا عَبْدُ اللهِ وَرَسُولُهُ

مسلم : كتاب الطهارة/ ٢٣٤

### DAY
# 122

**WHEN GOING TO THE MOSQUE**

O Allah, place light in my heart, light in my sight, light in my hearing, light on my right side, light on my left side, light above me, light below me, light in front of me, light behind me and magnify my light. Put light for me: light in my tongue, light in my sinews, light in my flesh, light in my blood, light in my hair, and place light in my self and magnify the light for me. O Allah, grant me light.

(M/AD)

### DAY
# 123

**WHEN ENTERING THE MOSQUE**

O Allah, open for me the doors of Your mercy.

(M)

## عند الذهاب إلى المسجد

اللَّهُمَّ اجْعَلْ فِى قَلْبِى نُورًا وَفِى بَصَرِى نُورًا وَفِى سَمْعِى نُورًا
وَعَنْ يَمِينِى نُورًا وَعَنْ يَسَارِى نُورًا وَفَوْقِى نُورًا وَتَحْتِى نُورًا
وَأَمَامِى نُورًا وَخَلْفِى نُورًا وَعَظِّمْ لِى نُورًا وَاجْعَلْ لِّى
نُورًا وَفِى لِسَانِىْ نُورًا وَفِى عَصَبِى نُورًا وَلَحْمِى نُورًا وَدَمِى
نُورًا وَشَعْرِى نُورًا وَبَشَرِى نُورًا وَاجْعَلْ فِى نَفْسِىْ نُورًا
وَأَعْظِمْ لِى نُورًا اللَّهُمَّ أَعْطِنِى نُورًا

مسلم: كتاب صلاة المسافرين/ ٧٦٣، أبو داوود: كتاب التطوع/ ١٣٥٣

## عند دخول المسجد

اللَّهُمَّ افْتَحْ لِى أَبْوَابَ رَحْمَتِكَ

مسلم: كتاب صلاة المسافرين/ ٧١٣

## DAY 124

#### WHEN ENTERING THE MOSQUE

J seek refuge in Allah the Almighty and in His noble Countenance and pre-eternal power from Satan the accursed.

(AD)

## DAY 125

#### WHEN LEAVING THE MOSQUE

O Allah, I ask of You Your favour.

(M)

**اليوم ١٢٤**

عند دخول المسجد

أَعُوذُ بِاللَّهِ الْعَظِيمِ وَبِوَجْهِهِ الْكَرِيمِ وَسُلْطَانِهِ الْقَدِيمِ مِنَ الشَّيْطَانِ الرَّجِيمِ

أبو داوود: كتاب الصلاة/ ٤٦٦

**اليوم ١٢٥**

عند الخروج من المسجد

اللَّهُمَّ إِنِّي أَسْأَلُكَ مِنْ فَضْلِكَ

مسلم: كتاب صلاة المسافرين/ ٧١٣

### DAY 126

WHEN LEAVING THE MOSQUE

In the name of Allah and peace be upon the Messenger of Allah; O Allah, forgive my sins and open for me the gates of your favour.

(IM)

### DAY 127

AFTER HEARING THE CALL TO PRAYER

O Allah, Lord of the perfect call and the prayer to be offered, grant Muhammad the means [of intercession], virtue, and raise him to the praiseworthy station which You have promised him.

(B)

### اليوم ١٢٦

**عند الخروج من المسجد**

بِسْمِ اللهِ وَالسَّلَامُ عَلَى رَسُولِ اللهِ اللَّهُمَّ اغْفِرْ لِى ذُنُوبِى
وَافْتَحْ لِى أَبْوَابَ فَضْلِكَ

ابن ماجه : كتاب المساجد/ ٧٥٥

### اليوم ١٢٧

**بعد سماع الأذان**

اللَّهُمَّ رَبَّ هَذِهِ الدَّعْوَةِ التَّامَّةِ وَالصَّلَاةِ الْقَائِمَةِ ءَاتِ مُحَمَّدًا
الْوَسِيلَةَ وَالْفَضِيلَةَ وَابْعَثْهُ مَقَامًا مَحْمُودًا الَّذِى وَعَدْتَهُ

البخاري : كتاب الأذان/ ٦١٤

**AFTER THE FIRST TAKBIR OF PRAYER**

*O* Allah, put a distance between me and my sins as You put a distance between east and west. O Allah, cleanse me of sins just as a white robe is cleansed of dirt. O Allah, wash away my sins with water, snow and hail.

(B/M)

**DAY 129**

**AFTER THE FIRST TAKBIR OF PRAYER**

*G* lory be to You, O Allah, all praise belongs to You, blessed is Your name, Your glory is exalted and there is no god except You.

(AD)

بعد تكبيرة الإحرام

اللَّهُمَّ بَاعِدْ بَيْنِي وَبَيْنَ خَطَايَاىَ كَمَا بَاعَدْتَ بَيْنَ الْمَشْرِقِ وَالْمَغْرِبِ، اللَّهُمَّ نَقِّنِي مِنَ الْخَطَايَا كَمَا يُنَقَّى الثَّوْبُ الْأَبْيَضُ مِنَ الدَّنَسِ، اللَّهُمَّ اغْسِلْ خَطَايَاىَ بِالْمَاءِ وَالثَّلْجِ وَالْبَرَدِ

البخاري: كتاب الأذان/ ٧٤٤، مسلم: كتاب المساجد/ ٥٩٨

بعد تكبيرة الإحرام

سُبْحَانَكَ اللَّهُمَّ وَبِحَمْدِكَ وَتَبَارَكَ اسْمُكَ وَتَعَالَى جَدُّكَ وَلَا إِلَهَ غَيْرُكَ

أبو داوود: كتاب الصلاة/ ٧٧٥

**DAY**
**130**

### To be recited in the tashahhud of the prayer

Peace and Allah's mercy and blessings be upon you, O Prophet.

(B/M)

**DAY**
**131**

### To be recited after tashahhud in the prayer

O Allah, I seek refuge in You from the chastisement of Hellfire and from the chastisement of the grave, from the trial of living and death and from the evil trial of the antichrist.

(M)

في جلوس التشهد

السَّلاَمُ عَلَيْكَ أَيُّهَا النَّبِيُّ وَرَحْمَةُ اللهِ وَبَرَكَاتُهُ

البخاري: كتاب الأذان/ ٨٣١، مسلم: كتاب الصلاة/ ٤٠٢

بعد التشهد

اللَّهُمَّ إِنِّي أَعُوذُ بِكَ مِنْ عَذَابِ جَهَنَّمَ وَمِنْ عَذَابِ الْقَبْرِ
وَمِنْ فِتْنَةِ الْمَحْيَا وَالْمَمَاتِ وَمِنْ شَرِّ فِتْنَةِ الْمَسِيحِ الدَّجَّالِ

مسلم: كتاب المساجد/ ٥٨٨

### Conveying blessings upon
### the prophet

O Allah, bless Muhammad and the household of Muhammad as You have blessed Ibrahim and the household of Ibrahim, You are indeed Most Praiseworthy, Most Glorious; and sanctify Muhammad and the household of Muhammad as You have sanctified Ibrahim and the household of Ibrahim, indeed You are Most Praiseworthy, Most Glorious.

(M)

### Conveying blessings upon
### the prophet

O Allah, send peace to Muhammad, his wives and offspring [or progeny] as You have sent peace to the household of Abraham; and bless Muhammad, his wives and offspring [or progeny] as You have blessed the household of Abraham, indeed You are All-Praiseworthy and All-Glorious.

(IS)

السلام على النبي

اللَّهُمَّ صَلِّ عَلَى مُحَمَّدٍ وَعَلَى ءالِ مُحَمَّدٍ كَمَا صَلَّيْتَ عَلَى ءالِ إِبْرَاهِيمَ إِنَّكَ حَمِيدٌ مَجِيدٌ اللَّهُمَّ بَارِكْ عَلَى مُحَمَّدٍ وَعَلَى ءالِ مُحَمَّدٍ كَمَا بَارَكْتَ عَلَى ءالِ إِبْرَاهِيمَ إِنَّكَ حَمِيدٌ مَجِيدٌ

مسلم: كتاب الصلاة/ ٤٠٦

السلام على النبي

اللَّهُمَّ صَلِّ عَلَى مُحَمَّدٍ وَأَزْوَاجِهِ وَذُرِّيَّتِهِ، كَمَا صَلَّيْتَ عَلَى ءالِ إِبْرَاهِيمَ، وَبَارِكْ عَلَى مُحَمَّدٍ وَعَلَى أَزْوَاجِهِ وَذُرِّيَّتِهِ، كَمَا بَارَكْتَ عَلَى ءالِ إِبْرَاهِيمَ إِنَّكَ حَمِيدٌ مَجِيدٌ

ابن السني: رقم الحديث: ٣٨٤

## DAY 134

O Allah, I seek refuge in You from the chastisement of the grave, and I seek refuge in You from the antichrist, and I seek refuge in You from the trial of living and the trial of death; O Allah, I seek refuge in You from committing sins and from loss.

(B)

## DAY 135

O Allah, I have greatly wronged my soul. Only You can forgive me, so grant me pardon out of Your grace; have mercy on me, for You are Most Forgiving, Most Merciful.

(B)

**بعد التشهد**

اللَّهُمَّ إِنِّي أَعُوذُ بِكَ مِنْ عَذَابِ الْقَبْرِ وَأَعُوذُ بِكَ مِنْ
فِتْنَةِ الْمَسِيحِ الدَّجَّالِ، وَأَعُوذُ بِكَ مِنْ فِتْنَةِ الْمَحْيَا وَفِتْنَةِ
الْمَمَاتِ، اللَّهُمَّ إِنِّي أَعُوذُ بِكَ مِنَ الْمَأْثَمِ وَالْمَغْرَمِ

البخاري : كتاب الأذان/ ٨٣٢

اليوم
١٣٥

**بعد التشهد**

اللَّهُمَّ إِنِّي ظَلَمْتُ نَفْسِي ظُلْمًا كَثِيرًا وَلاَ يَغْفِرُ الذُّنُوبَ
إِلاَّ أَنْتَ، فَاغْفِرْ لِي مَغْفِرَةً مِنْ عِنْدِكَ، وَارْحَمْنِي إِنَّكَ
أَنْتَ الْغَفُورُ الرَّحِيمُ

البخاري : كتاب الأذان/ ٨٣٢

**DAY
136**

O Allah, forgive me my past and future sins, the sins I kept hidden and those I committed openly, the sins of transgression and those ones which You Yourself know better than me; You are the Advancer and You are the Delayer; there is no god except You.

(M/T)

**DAY
137**

O Allah, I ask of You Paradise and seek refuge in You from the Fire.

(AD)

**بعد التشهد**

اللَّهُمَّ اغْفِرْ لِي مَا قَدَّمْتُ وَمَا أَخَّرْتُ وَمَا أَسْرَرْتُ
وَمَا أَعْلَنْتُ وَمَا أَسْرَفْتُ وَمَا أَنْتَ أَعْلَمُ بِهِ مِنِّي أَنْتَ
الْمُقَدِّمُ وَأَنْتَ الْمُؤَخِّرُ لَا إِلَهَ إِلَّا أَنْتَ

مسلم : كتاب صلاة المسافرين/ ٧٧١ ، الترمذي : كتاب الدعوات/ ٣٤٢١

**بعد التشهد**

اللَّهُمَّ إِنِّي أَسْأَلُكَ الْجَنَّةَ وَأَعُوذُ بِكَ مِنَ النَّارِ

أبو داوود : كتاب الصلاة/ ٧٩٢

**DAY 138**

### AFTER FINISHING THE PRAYER

*O* Allah, You are peace, and from You is peace. Blessed are You, O Possessor of glory and munificence.

(M)

**DAY 139**

### AFTER FINISHING THE PRAYER

*O* Allah, help me to remember You, be grateful to You and worship You in the best of manners.

(AD)

**اليوم ١٣٨**

**بعد التسليم**

اللَّهُمَّ أَنْتَ السَّلَامُ وَمِنْكَ السَّلَامُ تَبَارَكْتَ يا ذَا الْجَلَالِ وَالإِكْرَامِ

مسلم: كتاب المساجد/ ٥٩١

**اليوم ١٣٩**

**بعد التسليم**

اللَّهُمَّ أَعِنِّي عَلَى ذِكْرِكَ وَشُكْرِكَ وَحُسْنِ عِبَادَتِكَ

أبو داوود: كتاب الوتر/ ١٥٢٢

### DAY 140

#### AFTER FINISHING THE PRAYER

O Allah, I seek refuge in You from cowardice; I seek refuge in You from miserliness; I seek refuge in You from decrepitude; I seek refuge in You from the trial of this world; and I seek refuge in You from the chastisement of the grave.

(T)

### DAY 141

#### AFTER FINISHING THE PRAYER

O Allah, I seek refuge in You from disbelief, poverty and the chastisement of the grave.

(IS)

**بعد التسليم**

اللَّهُمَّ إِنِّي أَعُوذُ بِكَ مِنَ الْجُبْنِ وَأَعُوذُ بِكَ مِنَ الْبُخْلِ وَأَعُوذُ بِكَ مِنْ أَرْذَلِ الْعُمُرِ وَأَعُوذُ بِكَ مِنْ فِتْنَةِ الدُّنْيَا وَعَذَابِ الْقَبْرِ

الترمذي : كتاب الدعوات/ ٣٥٦٧

**بعد التسليم**

اللَّهُمَّ إِنِّي أَعُوذُ بِكَ مِنَ الْكُفْرِ وَالْفَقْرِ، وَعَذَابِ الْقَبْرِ

ابن السني : رقم الحديث ١١١

## DAY 142

Allah, guide me to righteous works and morals, for none guides to them except You, just as none drives away the worst of works and manners except You.

(TbMK)

## DAY 143

Allah, forgive all my sins and transgressions; O Allah, invigorate me, help me up, and guide me to righteous works and morals, for indeed none guides to them, nor drives away the worst of works and manners, except You.

(IS)

**اليوم ١٤٢**

**بعد التسليم**

اللَّهُمَّ اهْدِنِي لِصَالِحِ الْأَعْمَالِ وَالْأَخْلَاقِ ، فَإِنَّهُ لَا يَهْدِي لِصَالِحِهَا إِلَّا أَنْتَ ، وَلَا يَصْرِفُ سَيِّئَهَا إِلَّا أَنْتَ

الكبير للطبراني : جزء ٨ / رقم الحديث ٧٩٨٢

**اليوم ١٤٣**

**بعد التسليم**

اللَّهُمَّ اغْفِرْ لِي ذُنُوبِي وَخَطَايَايَ كُلَّهَا ، اللَّهُمَّ أَنْعِشْنِي ، وَاجْبُرْنِي ، وَاهْدِنِي لِصَالِحِ الْأَعْمَالِ وَالْأَخْلَاقِ ، إِنَّهُ لَا يَهْدِي لِصَالِحِهَا ، وَلَا يَصْرِفُ سَيِّئَهَا إِلَّا أَنْتَ

ابن السني : رقم الحديث ١١٦

### DAY
### 144

O Allah, Lord of Jibril, Israfil, Mika'il and Muhammad, may Allah's blessings and peace be upon him, I seek refuge in You from the Fire.

(IS)

### DAY
### 145

I seek forgiveness from Allah besides Whom there is no other deity, the Ever-Living, the Self-Subsistent, and I return to Him in repentance.

(IS)

**اليوم ١٤٤**

**بعد سنة الفجر**

اللَّهُمَّ رَبَّ جِبْرِيلَ، وَإِسْرَافِيلَ، وَمِيكَائِيلَ، وَمُحَمَّدٍ النَّبِيِّ صَلَّى اللهُ عَلَيْهِ وَسَلَّمَ، أَعُوذُ بِكَ مِنَ النَّارِ

ابن السني: رقم الحديث ١٠٣

**اليوم ١٤٥**

**بعد سنة الفجر أو الجمعة**

أَسْتَغْفِرُ اللهَ الَّذِى لَا إِلَهَ إِلَّا هُوَ الْحَىُّ الْقَيُّومُ وَأَتُوبُ إِلَيْهِ

ابن السني: رقم الحديث ٨٣

## DAY
## 146

O Allah, guide me among those whom You have guided; grant me well-being among those whom You have granted well-being; include me under Your custody among those whom You have included under Your custody; bless me in what You have given me and protect me from the evil of that which You have decreed, for You decree upon others and none decrees anything on You. Indeed, he whom you have taken under Your custody shall neither be humiliated, nor shall he whom You have declared enemity against gain any might; blessed and glorified are You, O our Lord!

(T/AD)

## دعاء القنوت

اللَّهُمَّ اهْدِنِي فِيمَنْ هَدَيْتَ وَعَافِنِي فِيمَنْ عَافَيْتَ وَتَوَلَّنِي
فِيمَنْ تَوَلَّيْتَ وَبَارِكْ لِي فِيمَا أَعْطَيْتَ وَقِنِي شَرَّمَا قَضَيْتَ
إِنَّكَ تَقْضِي وَلاَ يُقْضَىٰ عَلَيْكَ وَإِنَّهُ لاَ يَذِلُّ مَنْ وَالَيْتَ
وَلاَ يَعِزُّ مَنْ عَادَيْتَ تَبَارَكْتَ رَبَّنَا وَتَعَالَيْتَ

الترمذي : كتاب الصلاة/ ٤٦٤ ، أبو داوود : كتاب الوتر/ ١٤٢٥

### DAY
### 147

O Allah, I ask you beneficial knowledge, accepted works and a wholesome sustenance.

(IS)

### DAY
### 148

O Allah, through You do I strive, through You do I assail and through You do I fight.

(IS)

**اليوم ١٤٧**

بعد صلاة الفجر

اللَّهُمَّ إِنِّي أَسْأَلُكَ عِلْمًا نَافِعًا، وَعَمَلًا مُتَقَبَّلًا، وَرِزْقًا طَيِّبًا

ابن السني: رقم الحديث ١١٠

**اليوم ١٤٨**

بعد صلاة الفجر

اللَّهُمَّ بِكَ أُحَاوِلُ، وَبِكَ أُصَاوِلُ، وَبِكَ أُقَاتِلُ

ابن السني: رقم الحديث ١١٧

**DAY 149**

Allah, protect me from the Fire.

(AD)

**DAY 150**

Allah, this is Your night approaching and Your day receding and the voices of Your callers [calling Muslims to prayer], so forgive me.

(AD)

**اليوم ١٤٩**

بعد صلاة الفجر والمغرب

اللَّهُمَّ أَجِرْنِي مِنَ النَّارِ

أبو داوود: كتاب الأدب/ ٥٠٧٩

**اليوم ١٥٠**

عند أذان المغرب

اللَّهُمَّ هَذَا إِقْبَالُ لَيْلِكَ وَإِدْبَارُ نَهَارِكَ وَأَصْوَاتُ دُعَاتِكَ فَاغْفِرْ لِي

أبو داوود: كتاب الصلاة/ رقم الحديث ٥٣٠

157

**DAY 151**

### AFTER MAGHRIB PRAYER

You Who turns hearts around, confirm our hearts upon Your religion.

(IS)

**DAY 152**

### AFTER THE WITR PRAYER

Allah, I seek refuge in Your good pleasure from Your wrath, and in Your amnesty from Your punishment; and I seek refuge in You from You. I cannot encompass Your praise as You have praised Yourself.

(AD/T)

**اليوم ١٥١**

بعد صلاة المغرب

يَا مُقَلِّبَ الْقُلُوبِ ، ثَبِّتْ قُلُوبَنَا عَلَى دِينِكَ

ابن السني : رقم الحديث ٦٥٨

**اليوم ١٥٢**

في صلاة الوتر

اللَّهُمَّ إِنِّي أَعُوذُ بِرِضَاكَ مِنْ سَخَطِكَ وَبِمُعَافَاتِكَ مِنْ عُقُوبَتِكَ وَأَعُوذُ بِكَ مِنْكَ لاَ أُحْصِى ثَنَاءً عَلَيْكَ أَنْتَ كَمَا أَثْنَيْتَ عَلَى نَفْسِكَ

أبو داوود : كتاب الوتر/ ١٤٢٧ الترمذي : كتاب الدعوات/ ٣٥٦٦

IN TAHAJJUD PRAYER BEFORE
AL-FATIHAH

O Allah, Lord of Jibra'il, Mika'il and Israfil, Creator of the heavens and the earth, Knower of the unseen and the visible world, it is You Who judges between Your slaves regarding what they used to differ on; guide me by Your leave to what is right regarding what is differed about concerning the truth; indeed, You guide whosoever You will to a straight path.

(M/AD)

AFTER COMPLETING THE PRAYER
FOR GUIDANCE

O Allah, I ask You to show me what is best through Your knowledge, and bring it to pass through Your power, and I ask of You Your immense favour, for You are All-Powerful and I am not, You know and I do not, and You are the Knower of the Unseen. O Allah,

### في استفتاح صلاة التهجد

اللَّهُمَّ رَبَّ جِبْرَايِيلَ وَمِيكَايِيلَ وَإِسْرَافِيلَ فَاطِرَ السَّمَوَاتِ وَالْأَرْضِ عَالِمَ الْغَيْبِ وَالشَّهَادَةِ أَنْتَ تَحْكُمُ بَيْنَ عِبَادِكَ فِيمَا كَانُوا فِيهِ يَخْتَلِفُونَ اهْدِنِي لِمَا اخْتُلِفَ فِيهِ مِنَ الْحَقِّ بِإِذْنِكَ إِنَّكَ تَهْدِى مَنْ تَشَاءُ إِلَى صِرَاطٍ مُسْتَقِيمٍ

مسلم: كتاب صلاة المسافرين/ ٧٧٠، أبو داوود: كتاب الصلاة/ ٧٦٧

### دعاء الاستخارة

اللَّهُمَّ إِنِّي أَسْتَخِيرُكَ بِعِلْمِكَ، وَأَسْتَقْدِرُكَ بِقُدْرَتِكَ، وَأَسْأَلُكَ مِنْ فَضْلِكَ الْعَظِيمِ، فَإِنَّكَ تَقْدِرُ وَلَا أَقْدِرُ، وَتَعْلَمُ وَلَا أَعْلَمُ، وَأَنْتَ عَلَّامُ الْغُيُوبِ، اللَّهُمَّ إِنْ كُنْتَ تَعْلَمُ أَنَّ

if You know that this matter to be better for me in my religion, livelihood, and final end, then bring it about and facilitate it for me, and bless me with abundance therein. And if You know this matter to be worse for me in my religion, livelihood, and final end, then keep it from me, and keep me from it, and bring about the good for me whatever it may be, and make me pleased with it.

(B/AD)

DAY
155

## PROSTRATION DURING THE RECITATION OF THE QUR'AN

My face has prostrated to Him Who has created it and fashioned its hearing and sight through His might and power.

(T/AD)

هَذَا الأَمْرَ خَيْرٌ لِي فِي دِينِي وَمَعَاشِي وَعَاقِبَةِ أَمْرِي فَاقْدُرْهُ
لِي، وَيَسِّرْهُ لِي وَبَارِكْ لِي فِيهِ، وَإِنْ كُنْتَ تَعْلَمُ أَنَّ هَذَا
الأَمْرَ شَرٌّ لِي فِي دِينِي وَمَعَاشِي وَعَاقِبَةِ أَمْرِي فَاصْرِفْهُ عَنِّي
وَاصْرِفْنِي عَنْهُ، وَاقْدُرْ لِيَ الْخَيْرَ حَيْثُ كَانَ، ثُمَّ رَضِّنِي بِهِ

البخاري : كتاب الدعوات/ ٦٣٨٢ ، أبو داوود : كتاب الوتر/ ١٥٣٨

## في سجود التلاوة

سَجَدَ وَجْهِي لِلَّذِي خَلَقَهُ وَشَقَّ سَمْعَهُ وَبَصَرَهُ بِحَوْلِهِ وَقُوَّتِهِ

الترمذي : كتاب الصلاة/ ٥٨٠ ، أبو داوود : كتاب سجود القرآن/ ١٤١٤

### DAY 156

**WHEN BREAKING THE FAST**

O Allah, for You have I fasted and with Your sustenance do I break my fast.

(AD)

### DAY 157

**WHEN BREAKING THE FAST**

Praise be to Allah Who has helped me and so I fasted and provided me with sustenance with which I broke my fast.

(IS)

عند الإفطار من الصوم

اللَّهُمَّ لَكَ صُمْتُ وَعَلَىٰ رِزْقِكَ أَفْطَرْتُ

أبو داوود: كتاب الصوم/ ٢٣٦٠

عند الإفطار من الصوم

اَلْحَمْدُ لِلهِ الَّذِىْ أَعَانَنِيْ فَصُمْتُ وَرَزَقَنِيْ فَأَفْطَرْتُ

ابن السني: رقم الحديث ٤٧٩

**DAY 158**

### WHEN BREAKING THE FAST

O Allah, for You we have fasted, and with Your sustenance we have broken our fast, so accept it from us, for You are indeed All-Hearing, All-Knowing.

(IS)

**DAY 159**

### AFTER PUTTING ON THE PILGRIM'S GARMENTS

I am here at Your service, O Alah, I am here at Your service; You have no partners, I am here at Your service. Verily, all praise, blessings and dominion belong to You: You have no partners.

(B)

**اليوم ١٥٨**

عند الإفطار من الصوم

اَللَّهُمَّ لَكَ صُمْنَا وَعَلَى رِزْقِكَ أَفْطَرْنَا فَتَقَبَّلْ مِنَّا إِنَّكَ أَنْتَ السَّمِيعُ الْعَلِيمُ

ابن السني : رقم الحديث ٤٨٠

**اليوم ١٥٩**

ما يقوله الحاج إذا أحرم

لَبَّيْكَ اللَّهُمَّ لَبَّيْكَ، لَبَّيْكَ لاَ شَرِيكَ لَكَ لَبَّيْكَ، إِنَّ الْحَمْدَ وَالنِّعْمَةَ لَكَ وَالْمُلْكَ لاَ شَرِيكَ لَكَ

البخاري : كتاب اللباس / ٥٩١٥

### ON ENTERING THE GREAT
### MOSQUE OF MAKKAH

There is no god except Allah, alone without partners, to Him belongs the dominion and to Him belongs all praise, and He has power over all things.

(M)

### ON ENTERING THE GREAT
### MOSQUE OF MAKKAH

O Allah, this is Your sacred mosque and sanctuary, so make that the Fire is forbidden from touching me; grant me amnesty from Your chastisement when You resurrect Your slaves, and make me among Your closest servants and among those who obey You.

(N)

عند دخول الحرم المكي

لَا إِلَهَ إِلَّا اللهُ وَحْدَهُ لَا شَرِيكَ لَهُ، لَهُ الْمُلْكُ وَلَهُ الْحَمْدُ وَهُوَ عَلَى كُلِّ شَيْءٍ قَدِيرٌ

مسلم: كتاب الحج/١٢١٨

عند دخول الحرم المكي

اللَّهُمَّ هَذَا حَرَمُكَ وَأَمْنُكَ فَحَرِّمْنِي عَلَى النَّارِ وَأَمِّنِّي مِن عَذَابِكَ يَوْمَ تَبْعَثُ عِبَادَكَ، وَاجْعَلْنِي مِن أَوْلِيَائِكَ وَأَهْلِ طَاعَتِكَ

الأذكار: صفحة ١٦٤

### On seeing the ka'bah

O Allah, increase this House in glory, honour, grace and awe; and increase in glory, honour, goodness and awe whoever honours and glorifies it from among those who visit it for the greater or lesser pilgrimage.

(TbD)

### When standing between the black stone and the door of the ka'bah (al-multazam)

O Allah, verily You know what I have kept secret and what I have done openly, so accept my remorse; You also know what lies within me and what I have, so forgive my sins; You know my needs, so grant me what I ask for; O Allah, I ask You for a faith that permeates my heart,

عند رؤية الكعبة

اللَّهُمَّ زِدْ هَذَا الْبَيْتَ تَشْرِيفًا وَتَعْظِيمًا وَتَكْرِيمًا وَمَهَابَةً وَزِدْ
مَنْ شَرَّفَهُ وَكَرَّمَهُ مِمَّنْ حَجَّهُ وَاعْتَمَرَهُ تَشْرِيفًا وَتَكْرِيمًا
وَتَعْظِيمًا وَبِرًّا وَمَهَابَةً

الدعاء للطبراني : رقم الحديث ٨٥٤

**اليوم ١٦٣**

عند الوقوف بين الحجر الأسود والملتزم

اَللَّهُمَّ إِنَّكَ تَعْلَمُ سَرِيرَتِيْ وَعَلَانِيَتِيْ فَاقْبَلْ مَعْذِرَتِيْ وَتَعْلَمُ
مَا فِيْ نَفْسِيْ وَمَا عِنْدِىْ فَاغْفِرْ لِيْ ذُنُوْبِيْ وَتَعْلَمُ حَاجَتِيْ
فَأَعْطِنِيْ سُؤْلِيْ اللَّهُمَّ إِنِّيْ أَسْأَلُكَ إِيْمَانًا يُبَاشِرُ قَلْبِيْ ، وَيَقِيْنًا

and genuine certainty such that I know that nothing befalls me except what You have decreed for me, and such that I am content with what You have apportioned for me.

(TbMA)

### DAY
### 164

## WHEN STANDING BETWEEN THE BLACK STONE AND THE DOOR OF THE KA'BAH (AL-MULTAZAM)

O Allah, praise belongs to You in measure of all Your bounties and equal to all of Your increased blessings; I praise You by everything You deserve to be praised for, that which I know of and that which I do not know of, for all Your blessings, those I know of and those I do not know of; and I praise You in every circumstance.

(N)

صَادِقًا حَتَّى أَعْلَمُ أَنَّهُ لَا يُصِيبُنِي إِلَّا مَا كَتَبْتَ لِي، وَرِضًا بِمَا قَسَمْتَ لِي

الأوسط للطبراني : رقم الحديث ٥٩٧٤

**اليوم ١٦٤**

عند الوقوف بين الحجر الأسود والملتزم

اللَّهُمَّ لَكَ الْحَمْدُ حَمْدًا يُوَافِي نِعَمَكَ، وَيُكَافِئُ مَزِيدَكَ، أَحْمَدُكَ بِجَمِيعِ مَحَامِدِكَ مَا عَلِمْتُ مِنْهَا وَمَا لَمْ أَعْلَمْ عَلَى جَمِيعِ نِعَمِكَ مَا عَلِمْتُ مِنْهَا وَمَا لَمْ أَعْلَمْ، وَعَلَى كُلِّ حَالٍ

الأذكار : صفحة ١٦٦

### DAY 165

#### WHEN KISSING THE BLACK STONE

O Allah, [I do this] out of faith in You and out of firm belief in Your Book and in imitation of the practice of Your Prophet, may Allah's blessing and peace be upon him.*

(TbD)

*This was a prayer of 'Umar, may Allah be well pleased with him.

### DAY 166

#### WHEN GOING AROUND THE KA'BAH

Glory be to Allah and praise be to Allah; there is no god except Allah and Allah is great; and there is neither power nor might except through Allah.

(IM)

**عند تقبيل الحجر الأسود**

اللَّهُمَّ إِيمَانًا بِكَ ، وَتَصْدِيقًا بِكِتَابِكَ ، وَاتِّبَاعًا لِسُنَّةِ نَبِيِّكَ صَلَّى اللَّهُ عَلَيْهِ وَسَلَّمَ

الدعاء للطبراني : رقم الحديث ٨٦٠

**أثناء الطواف**

سُبْحَانَ اللهِ وَالْحَمْدُ لِلَّهِ وَلاَ إِلَهَ إِلاَّ اللهُ وَاللهُ أَكْبَرُ وَلاَ حَوْلَ وَلاَقُوَّةَ إِلاَّ بِاللهِ

ابن ماجه : كتاب المناسك / ٢٩٩٠

### DAY
### 167

##### When going around the ka'bah

O Lord, grant me contentment with what You have provided for me and bless me in it, and presently grant me a substitute for what I have missed and cannot possibly reach.

(H)

### DAY
### 168

##### When going around the ka'bah

O Allah, I seek refuge in You from doubt, polytheism, hypocrisy, discord and bad manners.

(S)

أثناء الطواف

رَبِّ قَنِّعْنِي بِمَا رَزَقْتَنِي، وَبَارِكْ لِي فِيهِ، وَاخْلُفْ عَلَى كُلِّ غَائِبَةٍ لِي بِخَيْرٍ

المستدرك : رقم الحديث ١٦٧٦

أثناء الطواف

اللَّهُمَّ إِنِّي أَعُوذُ بِكَ مِنَ الشَّكِّ وَالشِّرْكِ وَالنِّفَاقِ وَالشِّقَاقِ وَسُوءِ الْأَخْلَاقِ

نيل الأوطار : مجلد ٥/ صفحة ٥٧

### DAY 169

#### WHEN ENTERING THE HIJR

O Lord, I have come to You from a far-off place hoping for Your beneficence, so grant me of Your beneficence what will spare me from needing the beneficence of anyone besides You, O You Who is well known for beneficence!

(N)

### DAY 170

#### AT THE HILLOCK OF SAFA

Allah is great, Allah is great, Allah is great; there is no god except Allah, alone without any partners; to Him belong the dominion and praise and He has power over all things; there is no god except Allah alone; He has fulfilled His promise, aided His slave and alone defeated the confederates.

(M)

عند دخول الحجر

يَا رَبِّ أَتَيْتُكَ مِنْ شُقَّةٍ بَعِيدَةٍ مُؤَمِّلاً مَعْرُوفَكَ فَأَنِلْنِي

مَعْرُوفاً مِنْ مَعْرُوفِكَ تُغْنِينِي بِهِ عَنْ مَعْرُوفِ مَنْ سِوَاكَ

يَا مَعْرُوفاً بِالْمَعْرُوفِ

الأذكار: صفحة ١٦٦

على جبل الصفا

الله أَكْبَرُ الله أَكْبَرُ الله أَكْبَرُ لَا إِلَهَ إِلاَّ اللَّهُ وَحْدَهُ

لَا شَرِيكَ لَهُ لَهُ الْمُلْكُ وَلَهُ الْحَمْدُ وَهُوَ عَلَى كُلِّ شَيْءٍ

قَدِيرٌ، لَا إِلَهَ إِلاَّ اللَّهُ وَحْدَهُ أَنْجَزَ وَعْدَهُ وَنَصَرَ عَبْدَهُ وَهَزَمَ

الْأَحْزَابَ وَحْدَهُ

مسلم: كتاب الحج/ ١٢١٨

### DAY 171

WHEN PROCEEDING TOWARDS THE
HILLOCK OF MARWAH

O Lord, forgive and have mercy: indeed, You are the Most Mighty, the Most Noble.

(TbD)

### DAY 172

WHEN DRINKING THE WATER
OF ZAMZAM

O Allah, I ask You for beneficial knowledge, abundant sustenance and healing from all diseases.

(H)

## اليوم ١٧١

عند الذهاب نحو المروة

رَبِّ اغْفِرْ وَارْحَمْ إِنَّكَ أَنْتَ الْأَعَزُّ الْأَكْرَمُ

الدعاء للطبراني : رقم الحديث ٨٦٩

## اليوم ١٧٢

عند الشرب من زمزم

اللَّهُمَّ أَسْأَلُكَ عِلْمًا نَافِعًا، وَرِزْقًا وَاسِعًا، وَشِفَاءَ مِنْ كُلِّ دَاءٍ

المستدرك : كتاب المناسك/ ١٧٩١

## DAY 173

There is no god except God, to Him belong dominion and praise, He brings to life and causes death and He has power over all things.

(T)

## DAY 174

O Allah, my prayer, devotional acts, life and death are dedicated to You; to You is my return and my property is in fact Yours: O Allah, I seek refuge in You from the chastisement of the grave, from the whispering of the ego and from disconcertedness; O Allah, I seek refuge in You from the evil of that which is brought by the wind.

(T)

دعاء يوم عرفة

لَا إِلَهَ إِلَّا اللهُ وَحْدَهُ لَا شَرِيكَ لَهُ، لَهُ الْمُلْكُ وَلَهُ الْحَمْدُ
يُحْيِي وَيُمِيتُ وَهُوَ عَلَى كُلِّ شَيْءٍ قَدِيرٌ

الترمذي : كتاب الدعوات/ ٣٥٨٥

دعاء يوم عرفة

اللَّهُمَّ لَكَ صَلَاتِي وَنُسُكِي وَمَحْيَايَ وَمَمَاتِي وَإِلَيْكَ
مَآبِي وَلَكَ رَبِّ تُرَاثِي اللَّهُمَّ إِنِّي أَعُوذُ بِكَ مِنْ عَذَابِ
الْقَبْرِ وَوَسْوَسَةِ الصَّدْرِ وَشَتَاتِ الْأَمْرِ، اللَّهُمَّ إِنِّي أَعُوذُ
بِكَ مِنْ شَرِّ مَا يَجِيءُ بِهِ الرِّيحُ

الترمذي : كتاب الدعوات/ ٣٥٢٠

### On the day of 'arafah

O Allah, lead us by means of guidance; adorn us with Godfearingness and forgive us in the hereafter and in this world.

(TbD)

### When throwing pebbles during the hajj

O Allah, make that this pilgrimage is accepted and that [my] sins are forgiven.

(TbD)

**اليوم ١٧٥**

دعاء يوم عرفة

اللَّهُمَّ اهْـدِنَا بِالْهُدَى، وَزَيِّنَّا بِالتَّقْوَى، وَاغْـفِرْ لَنَا فِي الْآخِرَةِ وَالْأُولَى

الدعاء للطبراني : رقم الحديث ٨٧٨

**اليوم ١٧٦**

عند رمي الجمرات

اللَّهُمَّ اجْعَلْهُ حَجًّا مَبْرُورًا وَذَنْبًا مَغْفُورًا

الدعاء للطبراني : رقم الحديث ٨٨١

DAY
**177**

### WHEN SACRIFICING AN ANIMAL

J have turned my face to Him Who has created the heavens and earth, following the way of Ibrahim the upright, and I am not among those who associate partners with Allah. Verily, my prayer, devotional acts, life and death are dedicated to Allah, Lord of the worlds; He has no partners. Thus have I been commanded and I am the first to surrender to Him; in the name of Allah and Allah is great.

(AD)

DAY
**178**

### ON THE WAY TO THE EID PRAYER

A llah is great, Allah is great, Allah is great; there is no god except Allah, and Allah is great, Allah is great, and praise belongs to Him.

(N)

عند الأضحية

إنِّي وَجَّهْتُ وَجْهِيَ لِلَّذِي فَطَرَ السَّمَوَاتِ وَالأَرْضَ عَلَى مِلَّةِ إِبْرَاهِيمَ حَنِيفًا وَمَا أَنَا مِنَ الْمُشْرِكِينَ. إِنَّ صَلَاتِي وَنُسُكِي وَمَحْيَايَ وَمَمَاتِي لِلَّهِ رَبِّ الْعَالَمِينَ لَا شَرِيكَ لَهُ وَبِذَلِكَ أُمِرْتُ وَأَنَا مِنَ الْمُسْلِمِينَ. بِاسْمِ اللَّهِ وَاللَّهُ أَكْبَرُ

أبو داوود: كتاب الضحايا/ ٢٧٩٥

عند الذهاب إلى صلاة العيد

اللَّهُ أَكْبَرُ اللَّهُ أَكْبَرُ اللَّهُ أَكْبَرُ لَا إِلَهَ إِلَّا اللَّهُ، وَاللَّهُ أَكْبَرُ اللَّهُ أَكْبَرُ وَلِلَّهِ الْحَمْدُ

الأذكار: صفحة ١٤٦

**DAY 179**

### ON THE WAY TO THE EID PRAYER

Allah is immeasurably great, and praise be to Allah in abundance and glory be to Allah morning and evening.

(N)

**DAY 180**

### ON SIGHTING THE NEW MOON

Allah, let it [the new moon] appear with prosperity, faith, safety and state of surrender to You; my Lord and your Lord is Allah.

(T)

### عند الذهاب إلى صلاة العيد

اللَّهُ أَكْبَرُ كَبِيراً، وَالحَمْدُ لِلَّهِ كَثِيراً، وَسُبْحانَ اللَّهِ بُكْرَةً وأَصِيلاً

الأذكار : صفحة ١٤٦

### عند رؤية الهلال

اللَّهُمَّ أَهِلَّهُ عَلَيْنَا بِالْيُمْنِ وَالإِيمَانِ وَالسَّلَامَةِ وَالإِسْلَامِ رَبِّي وَرَبُّكَ اللَّهُ

الترمذي : كتاب الدعوات/ ٣٤٥١

### DAY 181

#### ON SIGHTING THE NEW MOON

Allah is great; praise be to Allah; there is no power or strength except through Allah. O Allah, I ask You for the good of this month and seek refuge in You from the evil of things destined and from the evil of the Mustering.

(A)

### DAY 182

#### WHEN IT IS HOT

There is no god except Allah, how hot is this day! O Allah, protect me from the heat of the Hell Fire.

(IS)

**اليوم ١٨١**

### عند رؤية الهلال

اللَّهُ أَكْبَرُ الْحَمْدُ لِلَّهِ لَا حَوْلَ وَلَا قُوَّةَ إِلَّا بِاللَّهِ اللَّهُمَّ إِنِّي أَسْأَلُكَ خَيْرَ هَذَا الشَّهْرِ وَأَعُوذُ بِكَ مِنْ شَرِّ الْقَدَرِ وَمِنْ سُوءِ الْحَشْرِ

أحمد : رقم الحديث ٢٢٧٩١

**اليوم ١٨٢**

### عند الحر الشديد

لَا إِلَهَ إِلَّا اللَّهُ، مَا أَشَدَّ حَرَّ هَذَا الْيَوْمِ، اللَّهُمَّ أَجِرْنِي مِنْ حَرِّ جَهَنَّمَ

ابن السني : رقم الحديث ٣٠٦

## DAY 183

### WHEN IT IS VERY COLD

There is no god except Allah, how cold is this day! O Allah, protect me from the extreme cold of Gehenna.

(IS)

## DAY 184

### FOR RAIN

O Allah, send us abundant, healthful, productive, beneficial and harmless rain, sooner rather than later.

(AD)

**اليوم ١٨٣**

عند البرد الشديد

لَا إِلَهَ إِلَّا اللهُ، مَا أَشَدَّ بَرْدَ هَذَا الْيَوْمِ، اللَّهُمَّ أَجِرْنِي مِنْ زَمْهَرِيرِ جَهَنَّمَ

ابن السني : رقم الحديث ٣٠٦

**اليوم ١٨٤**

الدعاء للمطر

اللَّهُمَّ اسْقِنَا غَيْثًا مُغِيثًا مَرِيئًا مُرِيعًا نَافِعًا غَيْرَ ضَارٍّ عَاجِلاً غَيْرَ آجِلٍ

أبو داوود : كتاب الاستسقاء/ ١١٦٩

### WHEN IT RAINS

*O* Allah, make these rain clouds beneficial!

(AD)

### WHEN THE WIND BLOWS

*O* Allah, I seek refuge in You from its evil.

(AD)

**اليوم ١٨٥**

عند المطر

اَللّٰهُمَّ صَيِّبًا نَافِعًا

أبو داوود: كتاب الأدب/ ٥٠٩٩

**اليوم ١٨٦**

إذا هبَّت الريح

اللّٰهُمَّ إِنِّي أَعُوذُ بِكَ مِنْ شَرِّهَا

أبو داوود: كتاب الأدب/ ٥٠٩٩

### DAY
### 187

#### When hearing thunder and seeing lightning

Allah, do not kill us through Your wrath, do not destroy us by means of Your chastisement and give us safety before that.

(T)

### DAY
### 188

#### During a storm

Allah, I ask You of its good, of the good that is in it and of the good for which it is sent; and I seek refuge in You from its evil, from the evil that is in it and from the evil for which it is sent.

(M)

عند الرعد والبرق

اللَّهُمَّ لَا تَقْتُلْنَا بِغَضَبِكَ وَلَا تُهْلِكْنَا بِعَذَابِكَ وَعَافِنَا
قَبْلَ ذَلِكَ

الترمذي : كتاب الدعوات/ ٣٤٥٠

عند العاصفة

اللَّهُمَّ إِنِّي أَسْأَلُكَ خَيْرَهَا وَخَيْرَ مَا فِيهَا وَخَيْرَ مَا أُرْسِلَتْ بِهِ
وَأَعُوذُ بِكَ مِنْ شَرِّهَا وَشَرِّ مَا فِيهَا وَشَرِّ مَا أُرْسِلَتْ بِهِ

مسلم : كتاب صلاة الاستسقاء/ ٨٩٩

DAY
**189**

### WHEN LEAVING HOME

O Allah, I seek refuge in You from going astray or being led astray; and from slipping or being made to slip, and from transgressing or being transgressed against, and from wronging others or being wronged by them.

(AD)

DAY
**190**

### WHEN LEAVING HOME

I n the name of Allah; I have put my trust in Allah; there is no power or strength except through Allah.

(AD)

**إذا غادر البيت**

اللَّهُمَّ إِنِّي أَعُوذُ بِكَ أَنْ أَضِلَّ أَوْ أُضَلَّ أَوْ أَزِلَّ أَوْ أُزَلَّ

أَوْ أَظْلِمَ أَوْ أُظْلَمَ أَوْ أَجْهَلَ أَوْ يُجْهَلَ عَلَيَّ

أبو داوود: كتاب الأدب/ ٥٠٩٤

**إذا غادر البيت**

بِسْمِ اللَّهِ تَوَكَّلْتُ عَلَى اللَّهِ لَا حَوْلَ وَلَا قُوَّةَ إِلاَّ بِاللَّهِ

أبو داوود: كتاب الأدب/ ٥٠٩٥

### WHEN LEAVING HOME ON A JOURNEY

O Allah, You are the Companion in the journey and Custodian of the family I have left behind; O Allah, I seek refuge in You from the discomfort of travel, from gloominess of sight, from the evil turn of events concerning my property and family, against turning from a good state to a bad state, from the supplication of a wronged person [against me], and also from the evil sight that one may encounter in one's family and property.

(M)

### WHEN SAYING FAREWELL
### TO A TRAVELLER

I entrust to Allah your religion, what you hold in trust and the works performed at the very end of life.

(AD/T)

عند السفر

اللَّهُمَّ أَنْتَ الصَّاحِبُ فِي السَّفَرِ وَالْخَلِيفَةُ فِي الأَهْلِ اللَّهُمَّ إِنِّي أَعُوذُ بِكَ مِنْ وَعْثَاءِ السَّفَرِ وَكَآبَةِ الْمَنْظَرِ وَسُوءِ الْمُنْقَلَبِ فِي الْمَالِ وَالأَهْلِ وَمِنَ الْحَوْرِ بَعْدَ الْكَوْنِ وَمِنْ دَعْوَةِ الْمَظْلُومِ وَمِنْ سُوءِ الْمَنْظَرِ فِي الأَهْلِ وَالْمَالِ

مسلم: كتاب الحج/ ١٣٤٢

إذا ودَّع مسافراً

أَسْتَوْدِعُ اللَّهَ دِينَكَ وَأَمَانَتَكَ وَخَوَاتِيمَ عَمَلِكَ

أبو داوود: كتاب الجهاد/ ٢٦٠٢، الترمذي: كتاب الدعوات/ ٣٤٤٣

### DAY
### 193

## WHEN SAYING FAREWELL
## TO A TRAVELLER

May Allah enrich you with Godfearingness, forgive your sins and make goodness easy for you wherever you are.

(T)

### DAY
### 194

## WHEN SAYING FAREWELL
## TO A TRAVELLER

May Allah enrich you with Godfearingness, direct you to goodness and save you from all worries.

(TbMK/IS)

اليوم
١٩٣

إذا ودَّع مسافراً

زَوَّدَكَ اللهُ التَّقْوَى وَغَفَرَ ذَنْبَكَ وَيَسَّرَ لَكَ الْخَيْرَ حَيْثُمَا كُنْتَ

الترمذي: كتاب الدعوات/ ٣٤٤٤

اليوم
١٩٤

إذا ودَّع مسافراً

زَوَّدَكَ اللهُ التَّقْوَى، وَوَجَّهَكَ فِي الْخَيْرِ، وَكَفَاكَ الْهَمَّ

الكبير للطبراني: جزء ١٢/ رقم الحديث ٣١٥١، ابن السني: رقم الحديث ٥٠٦

203

### DAY 195

**FOR SOMEONE STARTING A JOURNEY**

I put my trust in Allah Whose entrusted objects do not get lost.

(TbD)

### DAY 196

**FOR THE TRAVELLER**

O Allah, make the distance he traverses seem short and ease for him his travel.

(T)

اليوم
١٩٥

الدعاء للمسافر

أَسْتَوْدِعُكُمُ اللَّهَ الَّذِى لَا تَضِيعُ وَدَائِعُهُ

الدعاء للطبراني/ رقم الحديث : ٨٢٣

اليوم
١٩٦

الدعاء للمسافر

اللَّهُمَّ اطْوِ لَهُ الأَرْضَ وَهَوِّنْ عَلَيْهِ السَّفَرَ

الترمذي : كتاب الدعوات/ ٣٤٤٥

### In the morning while on a journey

O Allah, be our Companion and bestow Your favour upon us, and I seek refuge in Allah from the Fire.

(M)

### In the evening while on a journey

O earth! My Lord and your Lord is Allah; I seek refuge in Allah from your evil, from the evil in you, from the evil created in you, from the evil that moves about on you; and I seek refuge in Allah from lions, cobras, snakes, scorpions, from the inhabitants of earth and from Satan and his offspring.

(AD)

في صباح السفر

رَبَّنَا صَاحِبْنَا وَأَفْضِلْ عَلَيْنَا عَائِذًا بِاللَّهِ مِنَ النَّارِ

مسلم: كتاب الذكر و الدعاء/ ٢٧١٨

في مساء السفر

يَا أَرْضُ رَبِّي وَرَبُّكِ اللَّهُ أَعُوذُ بِاللَّهِ مِنْ شَرِّكِ وَشَرِّ مَا فِيكِ
وَشَرِّ مَا خُلِقَ فِيكِ وَمِنْ شَرِّ مَا يَدُبُّ عَلَيْكِ وَأَعُوذُ بِاللَّهِ
مِنْ أَسَدٍ وَأَسْوَدَ وَمِنَ الْحَيَّةِ وَالْعَقْرَبِ وَمِنْ سَاكِنِ الْبَلَدِ
وَمِنْ وَالِدٍ وَمَا وَلَدَ

أبو داوود: كتاب الجهاد/ ٢٦٠٣

### On boarding any vehicle

O Allah, we ask of You in this travel of ours righteousness and Godfearingness, and for works that You are pleased with; O Allah, make this journey easy for us and its distance seem short for us; O Allah, You are the Companion in the journey and Custodian of the family I have left behind; O Allah, I seek refuge in You from the discomfort of travel, from gloominess of sight, [and] from an evil turn of events concerning my property and family.

(M)

### On reaching a city

O Allah, Lord of the seven heavens and what they shade, and Lord of the earths and what they carry, and Lord of the satans and those whom they lead astray, and Lord of the winds

**إذا ركب**

اللَّهُمَّ إِنَّا نَسْأَلُكَ فِي سَفَرِنَا هَذَا الْبِرَّ وَالتَّقْوَى وَمِنَ الْعَمَلِ

مَا تَرْضَى ، اللَّهُمَّ هَوِّنْ عَلَيْنَا سَفَرَنَا هَذَا وَاطْوِ عَنَّا بُعْدَهُ ،

اللَّهُمَّ أَنْتَ الصَّاحِبُ فِي السَّفَرِ وَالْخَلِيفَةُ فِي الْأَهْلِ ، اللَّهُمَّ

إِنِّي أَعُوذُ بِكَ مِنْ وَعْثَاءِ السَّفَرِ وَكَآبَةِ الْمَنْظَرِ وَسُوءِ

الْمُنْقَلَبِ فِي الْمَالِ وَالْأَهْلِ

مسلم : كتاب الحج/ ١٣٤٢

**إذا وصل مدينة**

اللَّهُمَّ رَبَّ السَّمَوَاتِ السَّبْعِ وَمَا أَظْلَلْنَ، وَرَبَّ الْأَرَضِينَ

السَّبْعِ وَمَا أَقْلَلْنَ، وَرَبَّ الشَّيَاطِينِ وَمَا أَضْلَلْنَ، وَرَبَّ

and what they scatter around, we ask of You
the good of this city and the good of its
inhabitants, and seek refuge in You from its
evil and the evil of its inhabitants.

(TbD)

### On entering a city

O Allah, bless us in it; O Allah, bless us in it;
O Allah bless us in it. O Allah, grant us its
harvest, endear us to its inhabitants and
endear the righteous among its inhabitants
to us.

(TbD)

الرِّيَاحِ وَمَا ذَرَيْنَ، إِنَّا نَسْأَلُكَ خَيْرَ هَذِهِ الْقَرْيَةِ وَخَيْرَ أَهْلِهَا،
وَنَعُوذُ بِكَ مِنْ شَرِّهَا وَشَرِّ أَهْلِهَا وَشَرِّ مَنْ فِيهَا

الدعاء للطبراني : رقم الحديث ٨٣٨

### إذا دخل مدينة

اللَّهُمَّ بَارِكْ لَنَا فِيهَا، اللَّهُمَّ بَارِكْ لَنَا فِيهَا، اللَّهُمَّ بَارِكْ لَنَا فِيهَا،
اللَّهُمَّ ارْزُقْنَا جَنَاهَا، وَحَبِّبْنَا إِلَى أَهْلِهَا، وَحَبِّبْ صَالِحِى
أَهْلِهَا إِلَيْنَا

الدعاء للطبراني : رقم الحديث ٨٣٦

### DAY 202

ON RETURNING TO ONE'S HOMETOWN

There is no god except Allah, alone without partners, His promise is fulfilled, we repent, we worship [Allah alone] and our Lord do we praise.

(IAS)

### DAY 203

ON ENTERING ONE'S HOME

We return, we return [to Him] and to our Lord we repent, [may He] leave no sin on us.

(TbMK)

### عند الرجوع من السفر

لَا إِلَهَ إِلَّا اللَّهُ وَحْدَهُ صَدَقَ وَعْدَهُ تَايِبُونَ عَابِدُونَ لِرَبِّنَا حَامِدُونَ

مصنف ابن أبي شيبة : رقم الحديث ٢٩٦١٤

### عند دخول المنزل

أَوْبًا أَوْبًا، لِرَبِّنَا تَوْبًا، لَا يُغَادِرُ عَلَيْنَا حَوْبًا

الكبير للطبراني : جزء ١١/ رقم الحديث ١١٧٣٥

### DAY 204

#### On entering one's home

O Allah, I ask You for a good entry and a good leaving; in the name of Allah we enter and in the name of Allah we go out, and upon Allah, our Lord, we have placed our trust.

(AD)

### DAY 205

#### When the journey is over

Praise be to Allah through Whose might and majesty righteous deeds are accomplished.

(H)

**اليوم ٢٠٤**

عند دخول المنزل

اَللّٰهُمَّ إِنِّى أَسْأَلُكَ مِنْ فَجَأَةِ الْخَيْرِ وَأَعُوذُ بِكَ مِنْ فَجَأَةِ الشَّرِّ

ابن السني: رقم الحديث ٣٩

**اليوم ٢٠٥**

في نهاية الرحلة

الْحَمْدُ لِلّٰهِ الَّذِى بِعِزَّتِهِ وَجَلَالِهِ تَتِمُّ الصَّالِحَاتُ

المستدرك: رقم الحديث ٢٠٥١

**DAY 206**

(I begin) in the name of Allah, Most Compassionate, Most Merciful.
[If you forget at the beginning, say:]
In the name of Allah, at the beginning and at the end.

(AD/T)

**DAY 207**

ON TAKING FOOD

O Allah, bless us in what You have provided for us and protect us from the chastisement of the Fire; in the name of Allah.

(IS)

قبل الطعام

بِسْمِ اللهِ الرَّحْمَنِ الرَّحِيمِ
بِسْمِ اللهِ أَوَّلَهُ وَءَاخِرَهُ

أبو داوود: كتاب الأطعمة/ ٣٧٦٧ ، الترمذي: كتاب الأطعمة/ ١٨٥٨

عند تناول الطعام

اللَّهُمَّ بَارِكْ لَنَا فِيمَا رَزَقْتَنَا، وَقِنَا عَذَابَ النَّارِ بِسْمِ اللَّهِ

ابن السني: رقم الحديث ٤٥٧

### DAY 208

In the name of Allah, out of trust in Allah, and reliance on Him.

(AD/H)

### DAY 209

Praise be to Allah in abundance, Good and Glorified is He, He does not need anyone while He is sufficient unto His servants, He does not refuse anyone and none can do without Him, [He is] our Lord.

(B)

إذا أكل معه مريض

بِسْمِ اللهِ ثِقَةً بِاللهِ وَتَوَكُّلًا عَلَيْهِ

أبو داوود : كتاب الطب/ ٣٩٢٥، المستدرك : رقم الحديث ٧٢٧٦

بعد الطعام

الْحَمْدُ لِلَّهِ كَثِيرًا طَيِّبًا مُبَارَكًا فِيهِ، غَيْرَ مَكْفِيٍّ، وَلاَ مُوَدَّعٍ
وَلاَ مُسْتَغْنًى عَنْهُ، رَبَّنَا

البخاري : باب الأطعمة/ ٥٤٥٨

**DAY 210**

### AFTER FINISHING FOOD

Praise be to Allah Who has given us our sufficiency and drink, He does not need anyone while He is sufficient unto His servants and His blessing is acknowledged with gratitude.

(B)

**DAY 211**

### AFTER FINISHING FOOD

Praise be to Allah Who fed us, gave us drink and made us Muslims.

(AD)

**اليوم ٢١٠**

بعد الطعام

الْحَمْدُ لِلَّهِ الَّذِى كَفَانَا وَأَرْوَانَا، غَيْرَ مَكْفِىٍّ، وَلَا مَكْفُورٍ

البخاري : باب الأطعمة/ ٥٤٥٩

**اليوم ٢١١**

بعد الطعام

الْحَمْدُ لِلَّهِ الَّذِى أَطْعَمَنَا وَسَقَانَا وَجَعَلَنَا مُسْلِمِينَ

أبو داوود : كتاب الأطعمة/ ٣٨٥٠

## DAY 212

### After drinking water

Praise be to Allah Who has given us through His mercy sweet, fresh water to drink, and did not make it bitter, salty water due to our sins.

(TbD)

## DAY 213

### After drinking milk

O Allah, bless us in it and give us more of it.

(AD)

## اليوم ٢١٢

**بعد الشرب**

الْحَمْدُ لِلَّهِ الَّذِى سَقَانَا عَذْبًا فُرَاتًا بِرَحْمَتِهِ ، وَلَمْ يَجْعَلْهُ مِلْحًا أُجَاجًا بِذُنُوبِنَا

الدعاء للطبراني : رقم الحديث ٨٩٩

## اليوم ٢١٣

**بعد شرب الحليب**

اللَّهُمَّ بَارِكْ لَنَا فِيهِ وَزِدْنَا مِنْهُ

أبو داوود : كتاب الأشربة/ ٣٧٣٠

### DAY 214

#### AFTER EATING FRUIT

O Allah, bless us in our fruit crop, and bless us in our city, and bless us in our weights and measures.*

(M)

*literally, *sa'* and *mudd*, the measuring units.

### DAY 215

#### WHEN WASHING HANDS AFTER TAKING FOOD

Praise be to Allah Who feeds and is not fed: He has bestowed His favour upon us by guiding us, feeding us and giving us drink, and gifted us with all kinds of blessings.

(IS)

اليوم
٢١٤

### بعد أكل الفاكهة

اللَّهُمَّ بَارِكْ لَنَا فِى ثَمَرِنَا وَبَارِكْ لَنَا فِى مَدِينَتِنَا وَبَارِكْ لَنَا فِى صَاعِنَا وَبَارِكْ لَنَا فِى مُدِّنَا

مسلم : كتاب الحج/ ١٣٧٣

اليوم
٢١٥

### عند غسل اليدين بعد الطعام

الْحَمْدُ لِلَّهِ الَّذِى يُطْعِمُ وَلَا يُطْعَمُ، مَنَّ عَلَيْنَا فَهَدَانَا، وَأَطْعَمَنَا وَسَقَانَا، وَكُلَّ بَلَاءٍ حَسَنٍ أَبْلَانَا

ابن السني : رقم الحديث ٤٨٥

## DAY 216

### PRAYING FOR ONE'S HOST FOR THE FOOD GIVEN

Allah, bless them in what You have provided them, forgive them and have mercy on them.

(M)

## DAY 217

### PRAYING ONE'S HOST FOR THE FOOD GIVEN

Allah, feed him who has fed me and give drink to him who has given me to drink.

(M)

الدعاء لمن قدَّم الطعام

اللَّهُمَّ بَارِكْ لَهُمْ فِي مَا رَزَقْتَهُمْ وَاغْفِرْ لَهُمْ وَارْحَمْهُمْ

مسلم: كتاب الأشربة/ ٢٠٤٢

الدعاء لمن قدَّم الطعام

اللَّهُمَّ أَطْعِمْ مَنْ أَطْعَمَنِي وَأَسْقِ مَنْ أَسْقَانِي

مسلم: كتاب الأشربة/ ٢٠٥٥

**DAY 218**

### WHEN PUTTING ON NEW CLOTHING

Praise be to Allah who has clothed me with that which conceals my nudity and adorns me in my life.

(T)

**DAY 219**

### WHEN PUTTING ON NEW CLOTHING

O Allah, praise belongs to You, it is You Who has clothed me with it; I ask You for the good of it and the good that it is made for, and I seek refuge in You from its evil and from the evil it is made for.

(T)

**إِذَا لَبِسَ ثَوْباً جَدِيداً**

الْحَمْدُ لِلَّهِ الَّذِى كَسَانِى مَا أُوَارِى بِهِ عَوْرَتِى وَأَتَجَمَّلُ بِهِ فِى حَيَاتِى

الترمذي : كتاب الدعوات/ ٣٥٦٠

**إِذَا لَبِسَ ثَوْباً جَدِيداً**

اللَّهُمَّ لَكَ الْحَمْدُ أَنْتَ كَسَوْتَنِيهِ أَسْأَلُكَ مِنْ خَيْرِهِ وَخَيْرِ مَا صُنِعَ لَهُ وَأَعُوذُ بِكَ مِنْ شَرِّهِ وَشَرِّ مَا صُنِعَ لَهُ

الترمذي : كتاب اللباس/ ١٧٦٧ ، أبو داوود : كتاب اللباس/ ٤٠٢٠

### DAY 220

**WHEN DECIDING TO MARRY SOMEONE**

O Allah, You are All-Powerful and I am not, You know and I do not, and You are the Knower of the Unseen. [O Allah,] if You know that so-and-so is better for me in my religion, livelihood, and life to come, then choose her for me. And if You know that other than her is better for me in my religion, livelihood, and life to come, then choose her for me.

(H)

### DAY 221

**FOR THE NEWLY-MARRIED COUPLE**

May Allah bless and felicitate both of you and unite you both in goodness.

(AD)

**اليوم ٢٢٠**

إِذَا أَرَادَ أَنْ يَتَزَوَّجَ

اللَّهُمَّ إِنَّكَ تَقْدِرُ وَلَا أَقْدِرُ وَتَعْلَمُ وَلَا أَعْلَمُ، وَأَنْتَ عَلَّامُ

الْغُيُوبِ، فَإِنْ رَأَيْتَ لِي فُلَانَةَ خَيْرًا لِي فِي دِينِي وَدُنْيَايَ

وَءَاخِرَتِي، فَاقْدُرْهَا لِي، وَإِنْ كَانَ غَيْرُهَا خَيْرًا لِي مِنْهَا فِي

دِينِي وَدُنْيَايَ وَءَاخِرَتِي، فَاقْضِ لِي بِهَا

المستدرك : ١١٨٢

**اليوم ٢٢١**

الدُّعَاءُ لِلْعَرُوسَيْنِ

بَارَكَ اللَّهُ لَكَ وَبَارَكَ عَلَيْكَ وَجَمَعَ بَيْنَكُمَا فِي خَيْرٍ

أبو داوود : كتاب النكاح/ ٢١٣٣

## DAY 222

### ON ENTERING THE MARKET

In the name of Allah, O Allah, I ask of You the good of this marketplace and the good that is in it; and seek refuge in You from the evil of this market place and the evil that is in it; and I also seek refuge in You from uttering a false oath or incurring a losing deal.

(IS)

## DAY 223

### WHEN MEETING A FELLOW MUSLIM

We praise Allah and ask forgiveness for you.

(AD)

عند دخول السوق

بِسْمِ اللهِ، اللَّهُمَّ إِنِّي أَسْأَلُكَ مِنْ خَيْرِ هَذِهِ السُّوقِ وَخَيْرِ مَا فِيهَا، وَأَعُوذُ بِكَ مِنْ شَرِّ هَذِهِ السُّوقِ وَشَرِّ مَا فِيهَا، وَأَعُوذُ بِكَ أَنْ أُصِيبَ فِيهَا يَمِينًا فَاجِرَةً، أَوْ صَفْقَةً خَاسِرَةً

ابن السني : رقم الحديث ١٨١

إذا لقي مسلماً

نَحْمَدُ اللهَ وَنَسْتَغْفِرُ لَكُمْ

أبو داوود : كتاب الأدب/ ٥٢١١

**DAY 224**

O Allah, apportion for us fear of You that prevents us from committing acts of disobedience against You, and obedience to You by which You will enter us into Your Garden, and certitude that makes the afflictions of this world easy for us; and allow us to enjoy our hearing and sight for as long as we live, and avenge us against him who wrongs us, and support us against him who declares enmity against us, and do not afflict us in our religion nor make this world our greatest concern or the only thing that we know, and do not set on us him who does not show mercy to us.

(T)

**إِذَا قَامَ مِنَ المجلس**

اللَّهُمَّ اقْسِمْ لَنَا مِنْ خَشْيَتِكَ مَا تَحُولُ بِهِ بَيْنَنَا وَبَيْنَ مَعَاصِيكَ وَمِنْ طَاعَتِكَ مَا تُبَلِّغُنَا بِهِ جَنَّتَكَ وَمِنَ الْيَقِينِ مَا تُهَوِّنُ بِهِ عَلَيْنَا مُصِيبَاتِ الدُّنْيَا وَمَتِّعْنَا بِأَسْمَاعِنَا وَأَبْصَارِنَا وَقُوَّتِنَا مَا أَحْيَيْتَنَا وَاجْعَلْهُ الْوَارِثَ مِنَّا وَاجْعَلْ ثَأْرَنَا عَلَى مَنْ ظَلَمَنَا وَانْصُرْنَا عَلَى مَنْ عَادَانَا وَلَا تَجْعَلْ مُصِيبَتَنَا فِي دِينِنَا وَلَا تَجْعَلِ الدُّنْيَا أَكْبَرَ هَمِّنَا وَلَا مَبْلَغَ عِلْمِنَا وَلَا تُسَلِّطْ عَلَيْنَا مَنْ لَا يَرْحَمُنَا

الترمذي : كتاب الدعوات/ ٣٥٠٢

### DAY 225

##### WHEN CONCLUDING A MEETING

Glory be to You, O Allah, and all praise belongs to You; there is no god except You; I seek Your forgiveness and repent to You.

(T)

### DAY 226

##### ON SEEING SOMEONE IN A CALAMITY

Praise be to Allah Who has spared me from what He has tried you with and has preferred me greatly over many among those He has created.

(T)

**اليوم ٢٢٥**

إذا قام من المجلس

سُبْحَانَكَ اللَّهُمَّ وَبِحَمْدِكَ أَشْهَدُ أَنْ لَا إِلَهَ إِلاَّ أَنْتَ أَسْتَغْفِرُكَ وَأَتُوبُ إِلَيْكَ

الترمذي : كتاب الدعوات/ ٣٤٣٣

**اليوم ٢٢٦**

إذا رأى مبتلى

الْحَمْدُ لِلَّهِ الَّذِى عَافَانِى مِمَّا ابْتَلَاكَ بِهِ وَفَضَّلَنِى عَلَى كَثِيرٍ مِمَّنْ خَلَقَ تَفْضِيلا

الترمذي : كتاب الدعوات/ ٣٤٣١

**DAY**
**227**

### When facing financial difficulties

Allah, make me content with Your decree, bless me in that which is destined for me such that I do not like hastening what you have delayed or delaying what You have hastened.

(IS)

**DAY**
**228**

### For clearing debts and loans

Allah, grant me sufficiency in what You have made lawful such that I do not indulge in what is unlawful, and enrich me through Your favour such that I do not need anyone besides You.

(T)

**اليوم ٢٢٧**

### إذا عسرت المعيشة

اللَّهُمَّ رَضِّنِي بِقَضَائِكَ، وَبَارِكْ لِي فِيمَا قُدِّرَ لِي حَتَّى لَا أُحِبَّ تَعْجِيلَ مَا أَخَّرْتَ، وَلَا تَأْخِيرَ مَا عَجَّلْتَ

ابن السني : رقم الحديث ٣٥٠

**اليوم ٢٢٨**

### لقضاء الدَّين

اللَّهُمَّ اكْفِنِي بِحَلَالِكَ عَنْ حَرَامِكَ وَأَغْنِنِي بِفَضْلِكَ عَمَّنْ سِوَاكَ

الترمذي : كتاب الدعوات/ ٣٥٦٣

DAY
**229**

O Allah, Reliever of worry, Remover of anxiety, Responder to the calls of those under duress, the Merciful and Mercygiver in this world and in the hereafter, it is You Who will have mercy on me, so have mercy on me in a way that frees me from seeking the mercy of anyone else besides You.

(TbD)

DAY
**230**

O Allah, Master of the Kingdom, You give the Kingdom to whom You will, and seize the Kingdom from whom You will, You exalt whom You will, and You abase whom You will; in Your hand is the good: You are powerful over everything. You make the night to enter into the day and You make the day to enter into the night, You bring forth the living from

### لِقَضاءِ الدَّينِ

اللَّهُمَّ فَارِجَ الْهَمِّ، كَاشِفَ الْغَمِّ، مُجِيبَ دَعْوَةِ الْمُضْطَرِّينَ،
رَحْمَانَ الدُّنْيَا وَالْآخِرَةِ وَرحِيمَهُمَا، أَنْتَ تَرْحَمُنْي فَارْحَمْنِي
رَحْمَةً تُغْنِينِي بِهَا عَنْ رَحْمَةِ مَنْ سِوَاكَ

الدعاء للطبراني : رقم الحديث ١٠٤١

### لِقَضاءِ الدَّينِ

اللَّهُمَّ مَالِكَ الْمُلْكِ تُؤْتِي الْمُلْكَ مَنْ تَشَاءُ، وَتَنْزِعُ الْمُلْكَ
مِمَّنْ تَشَاءُ، وَتُعِزُّ مَنْ تَشَاءُ، وَتُذِلُّ مَنْ تَشَاءُ بِيَدِكَ الْخَيْرُ
إِنَّكَ عَلَىٰ كُلِّ شَيْءٍ قَدِيرٌ تُولِجُ اللَّيْلَ فِي النَّهَارِ وَتُولِجُ

the dead and You bring forth the dead from the living, and You provide for whomsoever You will without reckoning, O Merciful and Mercygiver in this world and the hereafter, You grant any of these to whom You will and withhold them from whom You will, have mercy on me such that I am freed from needing the mercy of anyone else besides You.

(TbMK)

DAY
231

O Allah, Lord of the heavens and earth and Lord of everything, You Who splits the grain and kernels of fruit, the Revealer of the Torah, Gospel, and the Qur'an, I seek refuge in You from the evil of any who possesses evil; it is You Who have him by the forelock. You are the First, there is nothing before You; You are the Last, there is nothing after You; You are the Outwardly Manifest, there is nothing above You; and You are the Inwardly Hidden, there is nothing below You; pay back for me my debt and spare me from poverty.

(AD)

النَّهَارَ فِى اللَّيْلِ، وَتُخْرِجُ الْحَىَّ مِنَ الْمَيِّتِ، وَتُخْرِجُ الْمَيِّتَ مِنَ الْحَىِّ، وَتَرْزُقُ مَنْ تَشَاءُ بِغَيْرِ حِسَابٍ رَحْمَـنَ الدُّنْيَا وَالْآخِرَةِ وَرَحِيمَهُمَا، تُعْطِى مَنْ تَشَاءُ مِنْهُمَا، وَتَمْنَعُ مَنْ تَشَاءُ، ارْحَمْنِى رَحْمَةً تُغْنِينِى بِهَا عَنْ رَحْمَةٍ مَنْ سِوَاكَ

الكبير للطبراني : جزء ٢٠/ صفحة ١٥٤

## اليوم ٢٣١

### عند دخول المسجد

اللَّهُمَّ رَبَّ السَّمَوَاتِ، وَرَبَّ الْأَرْضِ، وَرَبَّ كُلِّ شَىْءٍ، فَالِقَ الْحَبِّ وَالنَّوَى، مُنَزِّلَ التَّوْرَاةِ، وَالْإِنْجِيلِ، وَالْقُرْءانِ، أَعُوذُ بِكَ مِنْ شَرِّ كُلِّ ذِى شَرٍّ، أَنْتَ ءاخِذٌ بِنَاصِيَتِهِ، أَنْتَ الْأَوَّلُ فَلَيْسَ قَبْلَكَ شَىْءٌ، وَأَنْتَ الْآخِرُ فَلَيْسَ بَعْدَكَ شَىْءٌ، وَأَنْتَ الظَّاهِرُ فَلَيْسَ فَوْقَكَ شَىْءٌ، وَأَنْتَ الْبَاطِنُ فَلَيْسَ دُونَكَ شَىْءٌ، واقْضِ عَنِّى الدَّيْنَ، وَأَغْنِنِى مِنَ الْفَقْرِ

أبو داوود : كتاب الأدب/ باب مايقال عند النوم

### FOR PROTECTION AGAINST POVERTY

O Allah, I seek refuge in You from poverty, want and humiliation; and I seek refuge in You from wronging others or being wronged by them.

(AD)

### FOR PROTECTION AGAINST POVERTY

O Allah, You are the First such that there is nothing before You and You are the Last such that there is nothing after You, and You are the Outwardly Manifest such that there is nothing above You, and You are the Inwardly Hidden such that there is nothing beneath You, so pay our debt and free us from poverty.

(M)

للتعوذ من الفقر

اللَّهُمَّ إِنِّي أَعُوذُ بِكَ مِنَ الْفَقْرِ وَالْقِلَّةِ وَالذِّلَّةِ وَأَعُوذُ بِكَ مِنْ
أَنْ أَظْلِمَ أَوْ أُظْلَمَ

أبو داوود: كتاب الوتر/ ١٥٤٤

للتعوذ من الفقر

اللَّهُمَّ أَنْتَ الْأَوَّلُ فَلَيْسَ قَبْلَكَ شَيْءٌ وَأَنْتَ الْآخِرُ فَلَيْسَ
بَعْدَكَ شَيْءٌ وَأَنْتَ الظَّاهِرُ فَلَيْسَ فَوْقَكَ شَيْءٌ وَأَنْتَ الْبَاطِنُ
فَلَيْسَ دُونَكَ شَيْءٌ اقْضِ عَنَّا الدَّيْنَ وَأَغْنِنَا مِنَ الْفَقْرِ

مسلم: كتاب الذكر والدعاء/ ٢٧١٣

### FOR SOMEONE WHO HELPS ONE FINANCIALLY

May Allah bless you in your family and wealth.

(B)

### BEFORE SEXUAL INTERCOURSE

In the name of Allah; O Allah keep us away from Satan, and keep Satan away from what You have provided us.

(M)

الدعاء لمن قدَّم مساعدة مالية

بَارَكَ اللهُ لَكَ فِي أَهْلِكَ وَمَالِكَ

البخاري: كتاب البيوع/ رقم الحديث ٢٠٤٩

إذا أتى أهله

بِاسْمِ اللهِ، اللَّهُمَّ جَنِّبْنَا الشَّيْطَانَ، وَجَنِّبِ الشَّيْطَانَ مَا رَزَقْتَنَا

مسلم: كتاب النكاح/ ١٤٣٤

**DAY 236**

O Allah, from You and to You is the hair of so-and-so; in the name of Allah, and Allah is great.

(IAS)

**DAY 237**

I protect you by Allah's most perfect words from every satan and all vermin as well as from every reproachful eye.

(IS)

إذا عُقَّ عن المولود

اللَّهُمَّ مِنْكَ وَلَكَ عَقِيقَةُ فُلَانٍ، بِسْمِ اللهِ، اللَّهُ أَكْبَرُ

مصنف ابن أبي شيبة : رقم الحديث ٢٤٢٧١

لتعويذ الطفل

أُعِيذُكَ بِكَلِمَاتِ اللهِ التَّامَّةِ مِنْ كُلِّ شَيْطَانٍ وَهَامَّةٍ،
وَمِنْ كُلِّ عَيْنٍ لَامَّةٍ

ابن السني/ رقم الحديث ٦٣٤

**DAY 238**

FOR ONE WHO PRESENTS A GIFT

May Allah bless you.

(IS)

**DAY 239**

FOR PROTECTION AGAINST AN
EVIL NEIGHBOUR

O Allah, I seek refuge in You from an evil neighbour in the everlasting abode [the Afterlife].

(TbD)

اليوم ٢٣٨

الدعاء لمن أهدى إليك هدية

بَارَكَ اللهُ فِيكُمْ

ابن السني : رقم الحديث ٢٧٨

اليوم ٢٣٩

التعوذ من جار السوء

اللَّهُمَّ إِنِّي أَعُوذُ بِكَ مِنْ جَارِ السُّوءِ فِي دَارِ الْمُقَامَةِ

الدعاء للطبراني : رقم الحديث ١٣٤٠

### DAY 240

#### FOR PROTECTION AGAINST AN EVIL NEIGHBOUR

O Allah, I seek refuge in You from an evil day, from an evil night, from an evil hour, from an evil companion and from an evil neighbour in the Afterlife.

(TbD)

### DAY 241

#### WHEN SNEEZING

Praise be to Allah in all circumstances.

(AD)

**التعوذ من جار السوء**

اللَّهُمَّ إِنِّي أَعُوذُ بِكَ مِنْ يَوْمِ السُّوءِ، وَمِنْ لَيْلَةِ السُّوءِ، وَمِنْ سَاعَةِ السُّوءِ، وَمِنْ صَاحِبِ السُّوءِ، وَمِنْ جَارِ السُّوءِ فِي دَارِ الْمُقَامَةِ

الدعاء للطبراني : رقم الحديث ١٣٣٨

**عند العطاس**

الْحَمْدُ لِلَّهِ عَلَى كُلِّ حَالٍ

أبو داوود : كتاب الأدب/ ٥٠٣٣

### DAY 242

May Allah always keep you smiling.*

(B)

*Said by 'Umar, may Allah be well pleased with him,
when he saw the Prophet laughing; tradition relates
that his blessed laughter was a broad smile.

### DAY 243

Never mind, it is a [form of] purification,
Allah willing.

(B)

اليوم
٢٤٢

إذا رأى الابتسامة في وجه أخيه

أَضْحَكَ اللهُ سِنَّكَ

البخاري : كتاب الفضائل/ رقم الحديث ٣٦٨٣

اليوم
٢٤٣

الدعاء للمريض

لاَ بَأْسَ طَهُورٌ إِنْ شَاءَ اللهُ

البخاري : كتاب المرضى/ ٥٦٥٦

### DAY 244

#### SEEKING PROTECTION FOR SERIOUS DISEASES

O Allah, I seek refuge in You from leucoderma,* madness, leprosy and all serious diseases.

(AD)

*A skin disease characterized by white spots or patches on the body.

### DAY 245

#### FOR CURE AND RECOVERY

O Clement, O Generous, heal so-and-so.

(IAS)

التعوذ من الأمراض

اللَّهُمَّ إِنِّي أَعُوذُ بِكَ مِنَ الْبَرَصِ وَالْجُنُونِ وَالْجُذَامِ وَمِنْ سَيِّءِ الْأَسْقَامِ

أبو داوود : كتاب الوتر / ١٥٥٤

للشفاء من المرض

يَا حَلِيمُ، يَا كَرِيمُ، اشْفِ فُلَانًا

مصنف ابن أبي شيبة : رقم الحديث ٢٣٥٨٢

### FOR CURE AND RECOVERY

here is no god except You, glory be to You, verily I am of the wrongdoers.

(T)

### FOR CURING EYE DISEASE

Allah, let my sight gratify me and make me enjoy it for as long as I live; and avenge me against my enemy and aid me against the one who wrongs me.

(H)

**اليوم**
**٢٤٦**

**للشفاء من المرض**

لاَ إِلَهَ إِلاَّ أَنْتَ سُبْحَانَكَ إِنِّي كُنْتُ مِنَ الظَّالِمِينَ

الترمذي : كتاب الدعوات/ ٣٥٠٥

**اليوم**
**٢٤٧**

**لشفاء البصر**

اللَّهُمَّ مَتِّعْنِي بِبَصَرِي ، وَاجْعَلْهُ الْوَارِثَ مِنِّي ، وَأَرِنِي فِي
الْعَدُوِّ ثَأْرِي ، وَانْصُرْنِي عَلَى مَنْ ظَلَمَنِي

المستدرك : رقم الحديث ٨٣٤١

### For a urinary problem

Our Lord, Allah, Who is in heaven, hallowed is Your name; Your command is in the heaven and earth; just as Your mercy is in heaven, place Your mercy on earth; forgive our transgressions and sins, You are Lord of the goodly ones, send of Your mercy and healing upon this pain.

(AD)

### For alleviating fever

In the name of Allah, the Great, I seek refuge in Allah the Almighty from the evil of any vociferous fever and from the evil of the heat of the Fire.

(T)

**اليوم ٢٤٨**

لمشكلة التبول

رَبَّنَا اللهُ الَّذِى فِى السَّمَاءِ تَقَدَّسَ اسْمُكَ، أَمْرُكَ فِى السَّمَاءِ وَالأَرْضِ كَمَا رَحْمَتُكَ فِى السَّمَاءِ فَاجْعَلْ رَحْمَتَكَ فِى الأَرْضِ، اغْفِرْ لَنَا حُوبَنَا وَخَطَايَانَا، أَنْتَ رَبُّ الطَّيِّبِينَ، أَنْزِلْ رَحْمَةً مِنْ رَحْمَتِكَ وَشِفَاءً مِنْ شِفَائِكَ عَلَى هَذَا الوَجَعِ

أبو داوود: كتاب الطب/ ٣٨٩٢

**اليوم ٢٤٩**

لتخفيف الحمّى

بِسْمِ اللهِ الكَبِيرِ أَعُوذُ بِاللهِ العَظِيمِ مِنْ شَرِّ كُلِّ عِرْقٍ نَعَّارٍ وَمِنْ شَرِّ حَرِّ النَّارِ

الترمذي: كتاب الطب/ ٢٠٧٥

**DAY 250**

### FOR A BURN

Remove the hurt, O Lord of mankind, and heal, for You are the Healer: there is no healing except Your healing.

(A)

**DAY 251**

### FOR COMFORTING A SICK PERSON

Remove the hurt, O Lord of mankind, and heal for You are the Healer; there is no healing save Your healing such that no disease is left [unhealed].

(B/M)

إذا أصابه حرق

أَذْهِبِ الْبَاسَ رَبَّ النَّاسِ وَاشْفِ أَنْتَ الشَّافِي لَا شِفَاءَ إِلَّا شِفَاؤُكَ

أحمد : رقم الحديث ١٨٢٧٦

لمواساة المريض

أَذْهِبِ الْبَاسَ رَبَّ النَّاسِ وَاشْفِ أَنْتَ الشَّافِي لَا شِفَاءَ إِلَّا شِفَاؤُكَ شِفَاءً لَا يُغَادِرُ سَقَمًا

البخاري : كتاب الطب/ ٥٧٤٣ ، مسلم : كتاب السلام/ ٢١٩١

**DAY 252**

### FOR COMFORTING A SICK PERSON

In the name of Allah I protect you from anything that is harming you and from the evil of every ego or resentfully envious eye; may Allah heal you; in the name of Allah I protect you.

(M)

**DAY 253**

### FOR COMFORTING A SICK PERSON

O so-and-so, may Allah heal your illness, forgive your sins, and grant you well-being in your religion and body until the end of your lifespan.

(IS)

**اليوم ٢٥٢**

لمواساة المريض

بِاسْمِ اللهِ أَرْقِيكَ مِنْ كُلِّ شَيْءٍ يُؤْذِيكَ، وَمِنْ شَرِّ كُلِّ نَفْسٍ
أَوْ عَيْنٍ حَاسِدٍ اللهُ يَشْفِيكَ بِاسْمِ اللهِ أَرْقِيكَ

مسلم: كتاب السلام/ ٢١٨٦

**اليوم ٢٥٣**

لمواساة المريض

يَا فُلَانُ شَفَى اللهُ عَزَّ وَجَلَّ سَقَمَكَ، وَغَفَرَ لَكَ ذَنْبَكَ،
وَعَافَاكَ فِي دِينِكَ وَجِسْمِكَ إِلَى مُدَّةِ أَجَلِكَ

ابن السني: رقم الحديث ٥٤٨

### DAY 254

#### FOR HELP IN OLD AGE

 Allah, increase my provision in my old age when my life is near its end.

(TbD)

### DAY 255

#### WHEN FACING DEATH

*O* Allah, aid me in the agony of death.

(T)

**اليوم ٢٥٤**

طلب العون عند الكبر

اللَّهُمَّ اجْعَلْ أَوْسَعَ رِزْقِكَ عَلَيَّ عِنْدَ كِبَرِ سِنِّي،
وَانْقِطَاعِ عُمُرِي

الدعاء للطبراني: رقم الحديث ١٠٤٩

**اليوم ٢٥٥**

إذا عاين سكرات الموت

اللَّهُمَّ أَعِنِّي عَلَى سَكَرَاتِ الْمَوْتِ

الترمذي: كتاب الجنائز/ ٩٧٨

DAY
256

### ON HEARING ABOUT SOMEONE'S DEATH

Verily, we belong to Allah, and verily to Him we shall return; O Allah, record him with You among those who have excelled, and place his register in the highest garden of Paradise, grant his family a substitute; neither deprive us of his reward nor send us trials after him.

(IS)

DAY
257

### PRAYING FOR A DEAD PERSON

O Allah, forgive so-and-so, raise his degree among those who are guided, be the custodian of those whom he leaves behind, and forgive us and him, O Lord of all worlds; O Allah, expand for him his grave and illumine it for him.

(M/AD)

### إذا سمع بوفاة شخص

إِنَّا لِلَّهِ وَإِنَّا إِلَيْهِ رَاجِعُونَ وَإِنَّا إِلَىٰ رَبِّنَا لَمُنْقَلِبُونَ، اللَّهُمَّ اكْتُبْهُ عِنْدَكَ مِنَ الْمُحْسِنِينَ، وَاجْعَلْ كِتَابَهُ فِي عِلِّيِّينَ، وَاخْلُفْهُ فِي أَهْلِهِ فِي الْغَابِرِينَ، وَلَا تَحْرِمْنَا أَجْرَهُ، وَلَا تَفْتِنَّا بَعْدَهُ

ابن السني : رقم الحديث ٥٦١

### الدعاء للميت

اللَّهُمَّ اغْفِرْ لِفُلَانٍ، وَارْفَعْ دَرَجَتَهُ فِي الْمَهْدِيِّينَ، وَاخْلُفْهُ فِي عَقِبِهِ فِي الْغَابِرِينَ، وَاغْفِرْ لَنَا وَلَهُ يَا رَبَّ الْعَالَمِينَ. اللَّهُمَّ افْسَحْ لَهُ فِي قَبْرِهِ وَنَوِّرْ لَهُ فِيهِ

مسلم: كتاب الجنائز/ ٩٢٠، أبو داوود: كتاب الجنائز/ ٣١١٨

**DAY 258**

O Allah, forgive me and him and grant me after him a good compensation.

(M)

**DAY 259**

Verily, to Allah belongs what He has taken to Himself and to Him belongs what He has given; and everything with Him is according to an appointed time.

(B/M)

**اليوم ٢٥٨**

دعاء العزاء

اللَّهُمَّ اغْفِرْ لِي وَلَهُ وَأَعْقِبْنِي مِنْهُ عُقْبَى حَسَنَةً

مسلم: كتاب الجنائز / ٩١٩

**اليوم ٢٥٩**

دعاء العزاء

إِنَّ لِلَّهِ مَا أَخَذَ وَلَهُ مَا أَعْطَى وَكُلُّ شَيْءٍ عِنْدَهُ بِأَجَلٍ مُسَمًّى

البخاري: كتاب الجنائز/ ١٢٨٤، مسلم: كتاب الجنائز/ ٩٢٣

### WHEN FACING A CALAMITY

Verily, we belong to Allah and verily to Him we shall return; O Allah, I seek Your reward for the affliction that has befallen me, and also a better compensation for it.

(M)

### A FUNERAL PRAYER

O Allah, forgive those who are alive and those who are dead among us, our young ones and our old ones, our men and women, those who are present and those who are absent. O Allah, those whom You keep alive among us, keep them alive in a state of faith; and those whom You cause to die among us, cause them to die upon Islam. O Allah, neither deprive us of his reward nor send us astray after him.

(AD)

إذا أصابته مصيبة

إِنَّا لِلَّهِ وَإِنَّا إِلَيْهِ رَاجِعُونَ اللَّهُمَّ أْجُرْنِي فِي مُصِيبَتِي وَأَخْلِفْ

لِي خَيْرًا مِنْهَا

مسلم: كتاب الجنائز/ ٩١٨

اليوم
٢٦١

دعاء الجنازة

اللَّهُمَّ اغْفِرْ لِحَيِّنَا وَمَيِّتِنَا وَصَغِيرِنَا وَكَبِيرِنَا وَذَكَرِنَا وَأُنْثَانَا

وَشَاهِدِنَا وَغَائِبِنَا اللَّهُمَّ مَنْ أَحْيَيْتَهُ مِنَّا فَأَحْيِهِ عَلَى الإِيمَانِ

وَمَنْ تَوَفَّيْتَهُ مِنَّا فَتَوَفَّهُ عَلَى الإِسْلَامِ. اللَّهُمَّ لَا تَحْرِمْنَا أَجْرَهُ

وَلَا تُضِلَّنَا بَعْدَهُ

أبو داوود: كتاب الجنائز/ ٣٢٠١

### A FUNERAL PRAYER

O Allah, forgive him, have mercy on him, grant him amnesty, pardon him, honour his abode, ease his entering, wash him with water, snow and hail, cleanse him just as a white garment is cleansed of filth, exchange for him an abode better than his abode, a family better than his family, a spouse better than his spouse, enter him into Paradise and protect him from the chastisement of the grave and the chastisement of the Fire.

(M)

### ON SEEING A COFFIN

There is no god except Allah, the Living Who dies not.

(N)

دعاء الجنازة

اللَّهُمَّ اغْفِرْ لَهُ وَارْحَمْهُ وَعَافِهِ وَاعْفُ عَنْهُ وَأَكْرِمْ نُزُلَهُ
وَوَسِّعْ مُدْخَلَهُ وَاغْسِلْهُ بِالْمَاءِ وَالثَّلْجِ وَالْبَرَدِ وَنَقِّهِ مِنَ
الْخَطَايَا كَمَا نَقَّيْتَ الثَّوْبَ الْأَبْيَضَ مِنَ الدَّنَسِ وَأَبْدِلْهُ دَارًا
خَيْرًا مِنْ دَارِهِ وَأَهْلاً خَيْرًا مِنْ أَهْلِهِ وَزَوْجًا خَيْرًا مِنْ زَوْجِهِ
وَأَدْخِلْهُ الْجَنَّةَ وَأَعِذْهُ مِنْ عَذَابِ الْقَبْرِ أَوْ مِنْ عَذَابِ النَّارِ

مسلم: كتاب الجنائز/ ٩٦٣

عند رؤية الكفن

لا إِلَهَ إِلاَّ اللَّهُ الْحَيُّ الَّذِى لا يَمُوتُ

الأذكار: صفحة ١٣٦

## DAY 264

### WHEN BURYING THE DEAD

In the name of Allah and by Allah and following the way of the Messenger of Allah.

(T)

## DAY 265

### WHEN BURYING THE DEAD

Out of the earth We created you, and We shall restore you to it, and bring you forth from it a second time.

(A)

اليوم
٢٦٤

عند دفن الميت

بِسْمِ اللهِ وَبِاللهِ وَعَلَى مِلَّةِ رَسُولِ اللهِ

الترمذي : كتاب الجنائز/ ١٠٤٦

اليوم
٢٦٥

عند دفن الميت

مِنْهَا خَلَقْنَاكُمْ وَفِيهَا نُعِيدُكُمْ وَمِنْهَا نُخْرِجُكُمْ تَارَةً أُخْرَى

أحمد : رقم الحديث ٢٢١٨٧

**DAY 266**

### On visiting a graveyard

Peace be upon you, inhabitants of these dwellings, from among the believers and Muslims, and verily, Allah willing, we shall join you; I ask Allah to grant us and you safety.

(M)

**DAY 267**

### On visiting a graveyard

Peace be upon you, O dwellers of the graves, may Allah forgive us and you; you have preceded us and we shall follow you [soon].

(T)

**اليوم ٢٦٦**

عند زيارة القبور

السَّلَامُ عَلَيْكُمْ أَهْلَ الدِّيَارِ مِنَ الْمُؤْمِنِينَ وَالْمُسْلِمِينَ وَإِنَّا

إِنْ شَاءَ اللهُ لَلَاحِقُونَ أَسْأَلُ اللهَ لَنَا وَلَكُمُ الْعَافِيَةَ

مسلم: كتاب الجنائز/ ٩٧٥

**اليوم ٢٦٧**

عند زيارة القبور

السَّلَامُ عَلَيْكُمْ يَا أَهْلَ الْقُبُورِ يَغْفِرُ اللهُ لَنَا وَلَكُمْ أَنْتُمْ

سَلَفُنَا وَنَحْنُ بِالْأَثَرِ

الترمذي: كتاب الجنائز/ ١٠٥٣

### DAY 268

#### ON VISITING A GRAVEYARD

Peace be upon the inhabitants of these dwellings, from among the believers and Muslims, may Allah have mercy upon those who have gone first as well as upon those who will follow later; and verily, Allah willing, we shall join you [soon].

(M)

### DAY 269

#### WHEN FACING A DIFFICULTY

O Allah, be gentle with me by easing all that is hard, for easing all that is hard is easy for You. And I also ask You for affluence and well-being in this world and in the world to come.

(TbMA)

**اليوم ٢٦٨**

عند زيارة القبور

السَّلَامُ عَلَى أَهْلِ الدِّيَارِ مِنَ الْمُؤْمِنِينَ وَالْمُسْلِمِينَ وَيَرْحَمُ
اللَّهُ الْمُسْتَقْدِمِينَ مِنَّا وَالْمُسْتَأْخِرِينَ وَإِنَّا إِنْ شَاءَ اللَّهُ
بِكُمْ لَلَاحِقُونَ

مسلم: كتاب الجنائز/ ٩٧٤

**اليوم ٢٦٩**

إذا عسر عليه شيء

اللَّهُمَّ الطُفْ لِي فِي تَيْسِيرِ كُلِّ عَسِيرٍ، فَإِنَّ تَيْسِيرَ كُلِّ عَسِيرٍ
عَلَيْكَ يَسِيرٌ، وَأَسْأَلُكَ الْيُسْرَ وَالْمُعَافَاةَ فِي الدُّنْيَا وَالْآخِرَةِ

الأوسط للطبراني: رقم الحديث ١٢٥٠

## DAY 270

### SEEKING ALLAH'S HELP AND SUPPORT

My Lord, help me and do not help anyone against me, support me and do not support anyone against me, devise for me and do not devise against me, guide me and ease for me my guidance, and assist me against him who wrongs me.

(AD)

## DAY 271

### WHEN IN NEED OF SOMETHING

Allah,) I ask You for the reasons of Your mercy, the resolution of Your forgiveness, gain from every righteous deed, safety from all sins; [O Allah,] do not leave any of my sins unforgiven, and no anxiety except that You remove it, nor any need, which You are pleased with, except that You fulfil it [for me], O Most Merciful among those who show mercy.

(T)

**لطلب العون من الله**

رَبِّ أَعِنِّي وَلاَ تُعِنْ عَلَيَّ وَانْصُرْنِي وَلاَ تَنْصُرْ عَلَيَّ وَامْكُرْ لِي وَلاَ تَمْكُرْ عَلَيَّ وَاهْدِنِي وَيَسِّرْ هُدَايَ إِلَيَّ وَانْصُرْنِي عَلَى مَنْ بَغَى عَلَيَّ

أبو داوود: كتاب الوتر/ ١٥١٠

**عند الحاجة**

أَسْأَلُكَ مُوجِبَاتِ رَحْمَتِكَ وَعَزَائِمَ مَغْفِرَتِكَ وَالْغَنِيمَةَ مِنْ كُلِّ بِرٍّ وَالسَّلاَمَةَ مِنْ كُلِّ إِثْمٍ لاَ تَدَعْ لِي ذَنْبًا إِلاَّ غَفَرْتَهُ وَلاَ هَمًّا إِلاَّ فَرَّجْتَهُ وَلاَ حَاجَةً هِيَ لَكَ رِضًا إِلاَّ قَضَيْتَهَا يَا أَرْحَمَ الرَّاحِمِينَ

الترمذي: كتاب الصلاة/ ٤٧٩

**DAY 272**

### WHEN SOMEONE BRINGS GOOD NEWS

May Allah bring you good tidings, O so-and-so, in this world and in the world to come, and may He grant you safety in this world and in the world to come.

(IS)

**DAY 273**

### WHEN SEEING SOMETHING GOOD

Praise be to Allah through whose blessings righteous deeds are accomplished.

(IS)

**اليوم ٢٧٢**

**عند البشارة**

بَشَّرَكَ اللَّهُ بِخَيْرٍ يا فُلانُ فِي الدُّنْيا والْأخِرَةِ، وَسَلَّمَكَ اللَّهُ فِي الدُّنْيا والْأخِرَةِ

ابن السني : رقم الحديث ٢٨٨

**اليوم ٢٧٣**

**إذا رأى مايحب**

الْحَمْدُ لِلَّهِ الَّذِى بِنِعْمَتِهِ تَتِمُّ الصَّالِحَاتُ

ابن السني : ٣٧٨

DAY
**274**

## WHEN SEEING SOMETHING BAD

Praise be to Allah in every circumstance.

(IS)

DAY
**275**

## AGAINST ANY BAD OMEN

O Allah, there is no good except Your good, and there is no omen except Your omen, and there is no god apart from You.

(A/TbMK/IS)

286

إذا رأى مايكره

الْحَمْدُ لله عَلَىٰ كُلِّ حَال

ابن السني : ٣٧٨

إذا تطير من شيء

اللهُمَّ لَا خَيْرَ إلَّا خَيْرُكَ وَلَا طَيْرَ إلَّا طَيْرُكَ، وَلَا إلٰهَ غَيْرُكَ

أحمد : رقم الحديث ٧٠٤٥، الكبير للطبراني : جزء ١٣/ رقم الحديث ٣٨،

ابن السني : رقم الحديث ٢٩٢

### FOR PROTECTION AGAINST BLACK MAGIC

J seek refuge in Allah's most perfect words from every devil and harmful thing as well as from every resentful, envious eye.

(B/AD)

### SEEKING PROTECTION FROM THE DEVILS AND EVIL

J seek refuge in Allah's most perfect words, which no righteous or profligate person can trespass, from the evil of what descends from the sky or ascends to it, and from the evil of what is dispersed in the earth or comes out of it, and from the evil of the trials of the night and day, and from the evil of anyone who knocks at night or during the day, except someone knocking with something good, O All-Merciful!

(TbMK/IS)

للتعوذ من السحر

أَعُوذُ بِكَلِمَاتِ اللهِ التَّامَّةِ مِنْ كُلِّ شَيْطَانٍ وَهَامَّةٍ، وَمِنْ كُلِّ عَيْنٍ لَامَّةٍ

البخاري : كتاب أحاديث الأنبياء/ ٣٣٧١، أبو داوود : كتاب السنة/ ٤٧٣٧

للتعوذ من الشياطين والشر

أَعُوذُ بِكَلِمَاتِ اللهِ التَّامَاتِ الَّتِي لَا يُجَاوِزُهُنَّ بَرٌّ وَلَا فَاجِرٌ مِنْ شَرِّ مَا يَنْزِلُ مِنَ السَّمَاءِ وَمَا يَعْرُجُ فِيهَا، وَمِنْ شَرِّ مَا ذَرَأَ فِي الْأَرْضِ وَمَا يَخْرُجُ مِنْهَا، وَمِنْ شَرِّ فِتَنِ اللَّيْلِ وَفِتَنِ النَّهَارِ وَمِنْ شَرِّ طَوَارِقِ اللَّيْلِ وَالنَّهَارِ إِلَّا طَارِقًا يَطْرُقُ بِخَيْرٍ يَا رَحْمَانُ

الكبير للطبراني : جزء ٤/ رقم الحديث ٣٨٣٨، ابن السني : رقم الحديث ٦٣٧

### DAY 278

#### FOR PROTECTION AGAINST ALL EVIL

O Allah, I seek refuge in You from the evil of my hearing, from the evil of my sight, from the evil of my tongue, from the evil of my heart and from the evil of my semen.

(AD)

### DAY 279

#### WHEN FACING AN ENEMY

O Allah, we hold You as a protection against them and we seek refuge in You from their evil.

(AD)

للتعوذ من الشرور

اللَّهُمَّ إِنِّي أَعُوذُ بِكَ مِنْ شَرِّ سَمْعِي وَمِنْ شَرِّ بَصَرِى وَمِنْ
شَرِّ لِسَانِي وَمِنْ شَرِّ قَلْبِي وَمِنْ شَرِّ مَنِيِّ

أبو داوود: كتاب الوتر/ ١٥٥١

عند مواجهة العدو

اللَّهُمَّ إِنَّا نَجْعَلُكَ فِي نُحُورِهِمْ وَنَعُوذُ بِكَ مِنْ شُرُورِهِمْ

أبو داوود: كتاب الوتر/ ١٥٣٧

### DAY 280

#### TO ALLEVIATE OPPRESSION

O Allah, be sufficient unto me regarding them in whatever way You will.

(M)

### DAY 281

#### TO AVERT HARM

Whatever Allah wills, there is no strength or power except through Allah.

(IS)

اليوم
٢٨٠

لرفع الظلم

اللَّهُمَّ اكْفِنِيهِمْ بِمَا شِئْتَ

مسلم : كتاب الزهد والرقائق/ رقم الحديث : ٣٠٠٥

اليوم
٢٨١

لدفع الآفات

مَا شَاءَ اللهُ، لَا قُوَّةَ إِلَّا بِاللهِ

ابن السني : رقم الحديث ٣٥٧

### DAY 282

#### WHEN SUFFERING

Verily, we belong to Allah and to Him we shall return; O Allah, I seek the reward You hold for my affliction, so reward me and replace it for me with that which is better.

(M/AD)

### DAY 283

#### WHEN FACING A DIFFICULTY

Allah is sufficient for us and what a wonderful Custodian He is; we rely on Allah.

(T)

**اليوم ٢٨٢**

### عند المعاناة

إِنَّا لِلَّهِ وَإِنَّا إِلَيْهِ رَاجِعُونَ، اللَّهُمَّ عِنْدَكَ احْتَسَبْتُ مُصِيبَتِى فَأْجُرْنِى فِيهَا وَأَبْدِلْنِى مِنْهَا خَيْرًا

مسلم: كتاب الجنائز/ ٩١٨، أبو داوود: كتاب الجنائز/ ٣١١٩

**اليوم ٢٨٣**

### إذا استصعب عليه أمر

حَسْبُنَا اللهُ وَنِعْمَ الْوَكِيلُ، عَلَى اللهِ تَوَكَّلْنَا

الترمذي: كتاب صفة القيامة/ ٢٤٣١

### DAY 284

##### WHEN FACING A DIFFICULTY

O Allah, nothing is easy except what You make easy; You can make, if You will, a hard ground smooth.

(IS)

### DAY 285

##### WHEN LOOKING FOR A LOST ITEM

O Allah, You Who returns what has been lost and guides from error, return to me what I have lost, by Your power and might, for it is of Your gifting and favour.

(TbMK)

**اليوم ٢٨٤**

إذا استصعب عليه أمر

اللَّهُمَّ لَا سَهْلَ إِلَّا مَا جَعَلْتَهُ سَهْلًا، وَأَنْتَ تَجْعَلُ الْحَزَنَ إِذَا شِئْتَ سَهْلًا

ابن السني: رقم الحديث ٣٥١

**اليوم ٢٨٥**

إذا فقد شيئاً

اللَّهُمَّ رَادَّ الضَّالَّةِ، وَهَادِيَ الضَّلَالَةِ تَهْدِيْ مِنَ الضَّلَالَةِ، أُرْدُدْ عَلَيَّ ضَالَّتِي بِقُدْرَتِكَ وَسُلْطَانِكَ، فَإِنَّهَا مِنْ عَطَائِكَ وَفَضْلِكَ

الكبير للطبراني: جزء ١٢/ رقم الحديث ١٣٢٨٩

## DAY 286

There is no god except Allah, the Almighty, the Clement; there is no god except Allah, Lord of the Mighty Throne; there is no god except Allah, Lord of the heavens and Lord of the earth and Lord of the noble Throne.

(B/M)

## DAY 287

Praise be to Allah, Lord of the worlds; O Allah, I seek refuge in You from the evil of Your servants.

(TbD)

**عند الكرب والشدائد**

لَا إِلَهَ إِلاَّ اللهُ الْعَظِيمُ الْحَلِيمُ لَا إِلَهَ إِلاَّ اللهُ رَبُّ الْعَرْشِ الْعَظِيمِ لَا إِلَهَ إِلاَّ اللهُ رَبُّ السَّمَوَاتِ وَرَبُّ الْأَرْضِ وَرَبُّ الْعَرْشِ الْكَرِيمِ

البخاري: كتاب الدعوات/ ٦٣٤٥، مسلم: كتاب الذكر والدعاء/ ٢٧٣٠

**عند الكرب والشدائد**

الْحَمْدُ لِلَّهِ رَبِّ الْعَالَمِينَ، اللَّهُمَّ إِنِّي أَعُوذُ بِكَ مِنْ شَرِّ عِبَادِكَ

الدعاء للطبراني: رقم الحديث ١٠١٨

### DAY 288

WHEN IN DISTRESS AND HARDSHIP

O Allah, it is Your mercy that I seek so do not consign me to my ego even for a glance of an eye, and reform all my states; there is no god except You.

(AD)

### DAY 289

WHEN IN DISTRESS AND HARDSHIP

O Living, O Self-Subsistent, I call upon Your mercy for help.

(T)

**اليوم ٢٨٨**

عند الكرب والشدائد

اللَّهُمَّ رَحْمَتَكَ أَرْجُو فَلاَ تَكِلْنِي إِلَى نَفْسِي طَرْفَةَ عَيْنٍ وَأَصْلِحْ

لِي شَأْنِي كُلَّهُ لاَ إِلَهَ إِلاَّ أَنْتَ

أبو داوود : كتاب الأدب/ ٥٠٩٠

**اليوم ٢٨٩**

عند الكرب والشدائد

يَا حَيُّ يَا قَيُّومُ بِرَحْمَتِكَ أَسْتَغِيثُ

الترمذي : كتاب الدعوات/ ٣٥٢٤

### DAY 290

#### WHEN IN FEAR

O Allah, we hold You as a protection against them and seek refuge in You from their evil.

(AD)

### DAY 291

#### WHEN IN FEAR

Allah is great; Allah is great than all His creation; Allah is mightier than that which I fear and am beware of. I seek refuge in Allah apart from Whom there is no god, He Who holds the seven heavens lest they fall on earth, except through His leave, from the evil of your slave so-and-so and his party and followers, from among the jinn and human beings. O my God, be my protector against their evil, Your praise is exalted, Your name blessed and there is no god except You.

(TbMK)

عند الخوف

اللَّهُمَّ إِنَّا نَجْعَلُكَ فِي نُحُورِهِمْ، وَنَعُوذُ بِكَ مِنْ شُرُورِهِمْ

أبو داوود : كتاب الصلاة/ ١٥٣٧

عند الخوف

اللهُ أَكْبَرُ، اللهُ أَكْبَرُ مِنْ خَلْقِهِ جَمِيعًا، اللهُ أَعَزُّ
مِمَّا أَخَافُ وَأَحْذَرُ أَعُوذُ بِاللهِ الَّذِى لَا إِلَهَ إِلَّا هُوَ، الْمُمْسِكِ
السَّمَاوَاتِ السَّبْعَ أَنْ تَقَعْنَ عَلَى الْأَرْضِ إِلَّا بِإِذْنِهِ، مِنْ شَرِّ
عَبْدِكَ فُلَانٍ وَجُنُودِهِ، وَأَتْبَاعِهِ مِنَ الْجِنِّ وَالْإِنْسِ، إِلَهِى كُنْ
لِى جَارًا مِنْ شَرِّهِمْ، جَلَّ ثَنَاؤُكَ، وَعَزَّ جَارُكَ، وَتَبَارَكَ
اسْمُكَ، وَلَا إِلَهَ غَيْرُكَ

الكبير للطبراني : جزء ١٠/ رقم الحديث ١٠٥٩٩

### WHEN IN FEAR

O Allah, Lord of the seven heavens and seven earths, protect me from the evil of the devils from among the jinn and human beings, lest one of them wrongs us or transgresses against us.

(TbD)

**DAY**
**293**

### WHEN FACING LONELINESS AND ANXIETY

G lory be to the Master, the Most Holy, Lord of the angels and the Spirit, You have glorified the heavens and earth with might and power.

(IS)

**اليوم ٢٩٢**

عند الخوف

اللَّهُمَّ رَبَّ السَّمَوَاتِ السَّبْعِ وَرَبَّ الْأَرَضِينَ السَّبْعِ، كُنْ لِي
جَارًا مِنْ شَرِّ شَيَاطِينِ الْجِنِّ وَالْإِنْسِ أَنْ يَفْرُطَ عَلَيَّ أَحَدٌ
مِنْهُمْ أَوْ أَنْ يَطْغَى

الدعاء للطبراني : رقم الحديث ١٠٨٥

**اليوم ٢٩٣**

عند الوحشة والقلق

سُبْحَانَ الْمَلِكِ الْقُدُّوسِ، رَبِّ الْمَلَائِكَةِ وَالرُّوحِ، جَلَّلْتَ
السَّمَوَاتِ وَالْأَرْضَ بِالْعِزَّةِ وَالْجَبَرُوتِ

ابن السني : رقم الحديث ٦٣٩

## DAY 294

##### FOR THE ALLEVIATION OF WORRIES

Glory be to Allah the Almighty.

(IS)

## DAY 295

##### FOR THE ALLEVIATION OF WORRIES

O Allah, I am Your slave, the son of Your maid-servant, my forelock is in Your Hand, Your judgement concerning me is concluded, Your decree regarding me is just; I ask You by every name that You have, with which You have called Yourself, or revealed in Your Book, or taught someone among Your created beings, or withheld in the Knowledge of the Unseen with You, to make the Qur'an the light of my breast, the gladness of my heart, the means by which my grief is removed, and my anxiety and worry are cleared.

(IS)

عند الهم والحزن

سُبْحَانَ اللهِ الْعَظِيمِ

ابن السني : رقم الحديث ٣٣٨

عند الهم والحزن

اَللَّهُمَّ إِنِّيْ عَبْدُكَ وَابْنُ أَمَتِكَ، نَاصِيَتِي بِيَدِكَ، مَاضٍ فِيَّ
حُكْمُكَ، عَدْلٌ فِيَّ قَضَاؤُكَ، أَسْأَلُكَ بِكُلِّ اسْمٍ هُوَ لَكَ،
سَمَّيْتَ بِهِ نَفْسَكَ، أَوْ أَنْزَلْتَهُ فِي كِتَابِكَ، أَوْ عَلَّمْتَهُ أَحَدًا
مِنْ خَلْقِكَ، أَوِ اسْتَأْثَرْتَ بِهِ فِي عِلْمِ الْغَيْبِ عِنْدَكَ، أَنْ
تَجْعَلَ الْقُرْءانَ نُورَ صَدْرِي، وَرَبِيعَ قَلْبِي، وَجَلَاءَ حُزْنِي،
وَذَهَابَ هَمِّي وَغَمِّي

ابن السني : رقم الحديث ٣٣٩

### DAY 296

SEEKING ALLAH'S PROTECTION

O Allah, I seek refuge in You from impotence and laziness, from cowardice and miserliness, from decrepitude and the chastisement of the grave. O Allah, grant my self Godfearingness and purify it for You are its Custodian and Master. O Allah, I seek refuge in You from knowledge which is of no benefit, from a heart without awe, from a self that is never satiated and from a supplication that is unanswered.

(M)

### DAY 297

SEEKING ALLAH'S PROTECTION

O Allah, I seek refuge in You from those sins that prevent the answering of my requests. O Allah, I seek refuge in You from those sins that stop sustenance. O Allah, I seek refuge in You from those sins that bring about Your wrath.

(TbD)

لطلب الإلتجاء من الله

اللَّهُمَّ إِنِّى أَعُوذُ بِكَ مِنَ الْعَجْزِ وَالْكَسَلِ وَالْجُبْنِ وَالْبُخْلِ وَالْهَرَمِ وَعَذَابِ الْقَبْرِ اللَّهُمَّ ءَاتِ نَفْسِى تَقْوَاهَا وَزَكِّهَا أَنْتَ خَيْرُ مَنْ زَكَّاهَا أَنْتَ وَلِيُّهَا وَمَوْلَاهَا اللَّهُمَّ إِنِّى أَعُوذُ بِكَ مِنْ عِلْمٍ لَا يَنْفَعُ وَمِنْ قَلْبٍ لَا يَخْشَعُ وَمِنْ نَفْسٍ لَا تَشْبَعُ وَمِنْ دَعْوَةٍ لَا يُسْتَجَابُ لَهَا

مسلم : كتاب الذكر والدعاء/ ٢٧٢٢

لطلب الإلتجاء من الله

اللَّهُمَّ إِنِّى أَعُوذُ بِكَ مِنَ الذُّنُوبِ الَّتِى تَمْنَعُ إِجَابَتَكَ ، اللَّهُمَّ إِنِّى أَعُوذُ بِكَ مِنَ الذُّنُوبِ الَّتِى تَمْنَعُ رِزْقَكَ ، اللَّهُمَّ إِنِّى أَعُوذُ بِكَ مِنَ الذُّنُوبِ الَّتِى تُحِلُّ النِّقَمَ

الدعاء للطبراني : رقم الحديث ١٣٨٥

### SEEKING ALLAH'S PROTECTION

O Allah, I seek refuge in You from miserliness; I seek refuge in You from cowardice; I seek refuge in You lest I become senile; I seek refuge in You from the trial of this world; and I seek refuge in You from the chastisement of the grave.

(B)

### SEEKING ALLAH'S PROTECTION

O Allah, I seek refuge in You from being buried under the debris of a falling edifice; I seek refuge in You from falling from a high place [or from falling into the depth of a pit]; I seek refuge in You from drowning, burning, and senility; and I seek refuge in You from being

لطلب الالتجاء من الله

اللَّهُمَّ إِنِّي أَعُوذُ بِكَ مِنَ الْبُخْلِ، وَأَعُوذُ بِكَ مِنَ الْجُبْنِ،
وَأَعُوذُ بِكَ أَنْ أُرَدَّ إِلَى أَرْذَلِ الْعُمُرِ وَأَعُوذُ بِكَ مِنْ فِتْنَةِ
الدُّنْيَا، وَأَعُوذُ بِكَ مِنْ عَذَابِ الْقَبْرِ

البخاري : كتاب الدعوات/ ٦٣٦٥

لطلب الالتجاء من الله

اللَّهُمَّ إِنِّي أَعُوذُ بِكَ مِنَ الْهَدْمِ وَأَعُوذُ بِكَ مِنَ التَّرَدِّي
وَأَعُوذُ بِكَ مِنَ الْغَرَقِ وَالْحَرَقِ وَالْهَرَمِ وَأَعُوذُ بِكَ أَنْ

touched by the devil at the moment of death;
and I seek refuge in You lest I die while
running away from fighting for Your sake;
and I seek refuge in You from dying by being
stung [by a poisonous creature].

(AD)

### FOR GODFEARINGNESS

O Allah, I ask You for good health, continence,
trustworthiness, good manners and acceptance of all things destined [for me].

(TbMK)

يَتَخَبَّطَنِي الشَّيْطَانُ عِنْدَ الْمَوْتِ وَأَعُوذُ بِكَ أَنْ أَمُوتَ فِي
سَبِيلِكَ مُدْبِرًا وَأَعُوذُ بِكَ أَنْ أَمُوتَ لَدِيغًا

أبو داوود: كتاب الوتر/ ١٥٥٢

اليوم
٣٠٠

لطلب التقوى

اللهُمَّ إِنِّي أَسْأَلُكَ الصِّحَّةَ، وَالْعِفَّةَ، وَالْأَمَانَةَ، وَحُسْنَ
الْخُلُقِ، وَالرِّضَى بِالْقَدَرِ

الكبير للطبراني: جزء ١٣/ رقم الحديث: ٦٠

### DAY 301

#### FOR GODFEARINGNESS

O Allah, grant me two eyes ever red with tears that water the heart with tears from Your fear before the tears turn into blood and the teeth into live coal.

(TbD)

### DAY 302

#### FOR PRESERVATION IN RELIGION

O Allah, preserve me with Islam while standing, preserve me with Islam while sitting, preserve me with Islam while sleeping and do not accept, regarding me, anyone who declares enmity towards me or is resentfully envious of me.
O Allah, I ask of You the good that is in Your Hand, and seek refuge in You from evil whose stores are in Your Hand.

(TbMK)

للتقوى

اللَّهُمَّ ارْزُقْنِي عَيْنَيْنِ هَطَّالَتَيْنِ تَشْفِيَانِ الْقَلْبَ بِذُرُوفِ الدَّمْعِ مِنْ خَشْيَتِكَ قَبْلَ أَنْ يَكُونَ الدَّمْعُ دَمًا وَالْأَضْرَاسُ جَمْرًا

الدعاء للطبراني : رقم الحديث ١٤٥٧

للمحافظة على الدين

اللَّهُمَّ احْفَظْنِي بِالْإِسْلَامِ قَائِمًا، وَاحْفَظْنِي بِالْإِسْلَامِ قَاعِدًا، وَاحْفَظْنِي بِالْإِسْلَامِ رَاقِدًا، وَلَا تُطِعْ فِيَّ عَدُوًّا وَلَا حَاسِدًا، اللَّهُمَّ إِنِّي أَسْأَلُكَ مِنْ كُلِّ خَيْرٍ خَزَائِنُهُ بِيَدِكَ، وَأَعُوذُ بِكَ مِنْ كُلِّ شَرٍّ خَزَائِنُهُ بِيَدِكَ

الدعاء للطبراني : ١٤٤٥

### FOR DOING GOOD

O Allah, I ask You [that You grant me success] to do good, to abstain from forbidden things, to love the poor and that You forgive me and have mercy on me. And if You wish to try any people, then take my life away while not being touched by trial. And I ask You for Your love, the love of whoever loves You, and the love of any work that draws me closer to loving You.

(T)

### FOR LOVING ALLAH

O Allah, grant me Your love and the love of him whose love will benefit me with You.

(T)

للعمل الصالح

اللَّهُمَّ إِنِّى أَسْأَلُكَ فِعْلَ الْخَيْرَاتِ وَتَرْكَ الْمُنْكَرَاتِ وَحُبَّ الْمَسَاكِينِ وَأَنْ تَغْفِرَ لِى وَتَرْحَمَنِى وَإِذَا أَرَدْتَ فِتْنَةَ قَوْمٍ فَتَوَفَّنِى غَيْرَ مَفْتُونٍ، وَأَسْأَلُكَ حُبَّكَ وَحُبَّ مَنْ يُحِبُّكَ وَحُبَّ عَمَلٍ يُقَرِّبُنِى إِلَىٰ حُبِّكَ

الترمذي : كتاب تفسير القرآن/ ٣٢٣٣

لحب الله

اللَّهُمَّ ارْزُقْنِى حُبَّكَ وَحُبَّ مَنْ يَنْفَعُنِى حُبُّهُ عِنْدَكَ

الترمذي : كتاب الدعوات/ ٣٤٩١

### FOR EXCELLENT CONDUCT

O Allah, I ask You firmness in the matter, and I ask You for resolute consciousness [in my actions], and I ask You to enable me to be grateful for Your blessings and to worship You in the best way, and I ask You for a truthful tongue and a sound heart. And I seek refuge in You from the evil of what You know; and I ask of You the good of what You know, and I ask Your forgiveness for what You know, for You are indeed the Knower of the Unseen.

(T)

### FOR EXCELLENT CONDUCT

O Allah, grant me success in that which You love and be pleased with [my] speech and works, [my] intention and guidance, [for] indeed You have power over all things.

(TbD)

**اليوم ٣٠٥**

للرشد وحسن التصرف

اللَّهُمَّ إِنِّى أَسْأَلُكَ الثَّبَاتَ فِى الْأَمْرِ وَأَسْأَلُكَ عَزِيمَةَ الرُّشْدِ وَأَسْأَلُكَ شُكْرَ نِعْمَتِكَ وَحُسْنَ عِبَادَتِكَ وَأَسْأَلُكَ لِسَانًا صَادِقًا وَقَلْبًا سَلِيمًا وَأَعُوذُ بِكَ مِنْ شَرِّ مَا تَعْلَمُ وَأَسْأَلُكَ مِنْ خَيْرِ مَا تَعْلَمُ وَأَسْتَغْفِرُكَ مِمَّا تَعْلَمُ إِنَّكَ أَنْتَ عَلَّامُ الْغُيُوبِ

الترمذي : كتاب الدعوات/ ٣٤٠٧

**اليوم ٣٠٦**

للرشد وحسن التصرف

اللَّهُمَّ وَفِّقْنِى لِمَا تُحِبُّ وَتَرْضَى مِنَ الْقَوْلِ وَالْعَمَلِ ، وَالنِّيَّةِ وَالْهُدَى ، إِنَّكَ عَلَى كُلِّ شَيْءٍ قَدِيرٌ

الدعاء للطبراني : رقم الحديث ١٤٥٤

**DAY**
**307**

### For good character

O Allah, just as You have refined my physical constitution, refine my manners.

(TbD)

**DAY**
**308**

### For seeking knowledge

O Allah, benefit me with what You have taught me, teach me what is beneficial for me and increase me in knowledge; praise be to Allah in all circumstances and I seek refuge in Allah from the state of the dwellers of the Fire.

(T)

لحسن الخلق

اللَّهُمَّ كَمَا حَسَّنْتَ خَلْقِي فَأَحْسِنْ خُلُقِي

الدعاء للطبراني/ رقم الحديث ١٤٠٧

لطلب العلم

اللَّهُمَّ انْفَعْنِي بِمَا عَلَّمْتَنِي وَعَلِّمْنِي مَا يَنْفَعُنِي وَزِدْنِي عِلْمًا
الْحَمْدُ لِلَّهِ عَلَى كُلِّ حَالٍ وَأَعُوذُ بِاللَّهِ مِنْ حَالِ أَهْلِ النَّارِ

الترمذي : كتاب الدعوات/ ٣٥٩٩

**DAY 309**

### Giving thanks to Allah

O Allah, make me patient and grateful; make me look small in my own eyes but great in the eyes of people.

(Hy)

**DAY 310**

### For receiving allah's bounties

O Allah, I am weak, so remove my weakness in striving for Your good pleasure; take my forelocks to that which is good, and make Islam my ultimate good pleasure. O Allah, I am weak, so strengthen me; I am lowly, so elevate me; I am poor, so enrich me.

(TbMA/H)

### لشكر الله

اَللَّهُمَّ اجْعَلْنِيْ صَبُوْرًا وَاجْعَلْنِيْ شَكُوْرًا، وَاجْعَلْنِيْ فِيْ
عَيْنِيْ صَغِيْرًا وَّفِيْ أَعْيُنِ النَّاسِ كَبِيْرًا

مجمع الزوائد : رقم الحديث ١٧٤١٢

### لطلب الجود والكرم

اللَّهُمَّ إِنِّيْ ضَعِيْفٌ فَقَوِّ فِيْ رِضَاكَ ضَعْفِيْ، وَخُذْ إِلَى الْخَيْرِ
بِنَاصِيَتِيْ، وَاجْعَلِ الْإِسْلَامَ مُنْتَهَى رِضَايِ، اللَّهُمَّ إِنِّيْ
ضَعِيْفٌ فَقَوِّنِيْ، وَإِنِّيْ ذَلِيْلٌ فَأَعِزَّنِيْ، وَإِنِّيْ فَقِيْرٌ فَأَغْنِنِيْ

الأوسط للطبراني : رقم الحديث ٦٥٨٥ ، المستدرك ١٩٨٣

### DAY
### 311

WHEN ANGRY

*O* Allah, Lord of Muhammad the Prophet, forgive my sins and remove the anger that is in my heart and protect me from the trials that lead astray for as long as You keep us alive.

(A)

### DAY
### 312

WHEN ANGRY

*J* seek refuge in Allah from Satan the accursed.

(B/M)

**اليوم ٣١١**

عند الغضب

اللهُمَّ رَبَّ مُحَمَّدٍ النَّبِيِّ اغْفِرْ لِي ذَنْبِي وَأَذْهِبْ غَيْظَ قَلْبِي وَأَجِرْنِي مِنْ مُضِلَّاتِ الْفِتَنِ مَا أَحْيَيْتَنَا

أحمد: رقم الحديث ٢٦٥٧٦

**اليوم ٣١٢**

عند الغضب

أَعُوذُ بِاللهِ مِنَ الشَّيْطَانِ الرَّجِيمِ

البخاري: كتاب الأدب/ ٦١١٥، مسلم: كتاب البر والصلة/ ٢٦١٠

### DAY 313

#### TO GET RID OF JEALOUSY

In the name of Allah; O Allah, cure me with Your cure, and heal me with Your healing, and make me through Your favour independent of everyone other than You, and keep away from me Your harm.

(IS)

### DAY 314

#### FOR PROTECTION AGAINST SIN

O Allah, to You have I surrendered and in You do I believe, upon You do I put my trust and to You do I repent and by means of You do I argue. O Allah I seek refuge in Your might, there is no god except You, lest You send me astray; You are the Living Who dies not while jinns and humans die.

(M)

## للتخلص من الغيرة

بِسْمِ اللَّهِ، اللَّهُمَّ دَاوِنِي بِدَوَائِكَ، وَاشْفِنِي بِشِفَائِكَ، وَأَغْنِنِي بِفَضْلِكَ عَمَّنْ سِوَاكَ، وَاحْذَرْ عَنِّي أَذَاكَ

ابن السني : رقم الحديث : ٦٢١

## للتعوذ من الذنب

اللَّهُمَّ لَكَ أَسْلَمْتُ وَبِكَ ءَامَنْتُ وَعَلَيْكَ تَوَكَّلْتُ وَإِلَيْكَ أَنَبْتُ وَبِكَ خَاصَمْتُ اللَّهُمَّ إِنِّي أَعُوذُ بِعِزَّتِكَ لَا إِلَهَ إِلَّا أَنْتَ أَنْ تُضِلَّنِي أَنْتَ الْحَيُّ الَّذِي لَا يَمُوتُ وَالْجِنُّ وَالْإِنْسُ يَمُوتُونَ

مسلم : كتاب الذكر والدعاء/ ٢٧١٧

### DAY 315

Allah, I seek refuge in You from discord, hypocrisy and bad manners.

(AD)

### DAY 316

FOR PROTECTION AGAINST GREED

Allah, I seek refuge in You from greed that will characterise me.

(TbD)

للتعوذ من سوء التصرف

اللَّهُمَّ إِنِّي أَعُوذُ بِكَ مِنَ الشِّقَاقِ وَالنِّفَاقِ وَسُوءِ الأَخْلاقِ

أبو داوود: كتاب الوتر/ ١٥٤٦

للتعوذ من الطمع

اَللَّهُمَّ إِنِّي أَعُوذُ بِكَ مِنْ طَمَعٍ يَهْدِىْ إِلَى طَبَعٍ

الدعاء للطبراني: رقم الحديث ١٣٨٨

## DAY 317

### WHEN REPENTING

O Allah, I repent to You because of it, and I will never commit it again.

(H)

## DAY 318

### FOR FORGIVENESS

O Allah, forgive my transgressions, ignorance, excesses in my affairs and what You know better than me. O Allah, forgive my over-seriousness and levity, my mistakes and intentional wrongs: all of which are in me. O Allah, forgive the sins I committed in the past and the sins I will commit in the future, those sins I committed in secret and those I committed openly, as well as those sins that You are more aware of than me; You are the Advancer and You are the Delayer and You are powerful over all things.

(M)

عند التوبة

اللَّهُمَّ إِنِّى أَتُوبُ إِلَيْكَ مِنْهَا لَا أَرْجِعُ إِلَيْهَا أَبَدًا

المستدرك : رقم الحديث ٧٧٥٤

للمغفرة

اللَّهُمَّ اغْفِرْ لِى خَطِيئَتِى وَجَهْلِى وَإِسْرَافِى فِى أَمْرِى

وَمَا أَنْتَ أَعْلَمُ بِهِ مِنِّى اللَّهُمَّ اغْفِرْ لِى جِدِّى وَهَزْلِى وَخَطَئِى

وَعَمْدِى وَكُلُّ ذَلِكَ عِنْدِى اللَّهُمَّ اغْفِرْ لِى مَا قَدَّمْتُ

وَمَا أَخَّرْتُ وَمَا أَسْرَرْتُ وَمَا أَعْلَنْتُ وَمَا أَنْتَ أَعْلَمُ بِهِ مِنِّى

أَنْتَ الْمُقَدِّمُ وَأَنْتَ الْمُؤَخِّرُ وَأَنْتَ عَلَى كُلِّ شَيْءٍ قَدِيرٌ

مسلم : كتاب الذكر والدعاء/ ٢٧١٩

**DAY 319**

*O* Allah, forgive all my sins: the subtle and obvious sins, those I committed secretly and those I committed openly, the first sin and the last sin.

(TbD)

**DAY 320**

*O* Allah, I repent to You from them [the sins I committed] and I will never return to them!

(TbD)

للمغفرة

اَللَّهُمَّ اغْفِرْ لِي ذَنْبِي كُلَّهُ، دِقَّهُ وَجِلَّهُ، وَعَلَانِيَتَهُ وَسِرَّهُ،
وَأَوَّلَهُ وَآخِرَهُ

الدعاء للطبراني : رقم الحديث ٦٠٧

اليوم
٣٢٠

للمغفرة

اَللَّهُمَّ إِنِّي أَتُوبُ إِلَيْكَ مِنْهَا لَا أَرْجِعُ إِلَيْهَا أَبَدًا

الدعاء للطبراني : رقم الحديث ٢٠٨

### For forgiveness

I ask forgiveness from Allah the Almighty apart from Whom there is no god, the Living, the Self-Subsistent, and I repent to Him.

(H)

### For forgiveness

O Allah, You are Most Forgiving, Generous and You like forgiveness so forgive me.

(T)

للمغفرة

أَسْتَغْفِرُ اللَّهَ الْعَظِيمَ الَّذِى لَا إِلَهَ إِلَّا هُوَ الْحَىُّ الْقَيُّومُ، وَأَتُوبُ إِلَيْهِ

المستدرك : رقم الحديث ١٩٣٦

اليوم
٣٢٢

للمغفرة

اللَّهُمَّ إِنَّكَ عَفُوٌّ كَرِيمٌ تُحِبُّ الْعَفْوَ فَاعْفُ عَنِّى

الترمذي : كتاب الدعوات/ ٣٥١٣

DAY
**323**

### FOR FORGIVENESS

O Allah, I ask You by Your mercy that encompasses all things to forgive me.

(IS)

DAY
**324**

### FOR FORGIVENESS

There is no god except Allah, alone without partners, to Him belongs the dominion and praise and He has power over all things: there is no power or strength except through Allah; glory be to Allah; praise be to Allah; there is no god except Allah; and Allah is great.

(IS)

للمغفرة

اللَّهُمَّ إِنِّى أَسْأَلُكَ بِرَحْمَتِكَ الَّتِى وَسِعَتْ كُلَّ شَىْءٍ أَنْ تَغْفِرَ لِى

ابن السني : رقم الحديث ٤٨١

**اليوم ٣٢٤**

للمغفرة

لَا إِلَهَ إِلَّا اللهُ، وَحْدَهُ لَا شَرِيكَ لَهُ، لَهُ الْمُلْكُ، وَلَهُ الْحَمْدُ، وَهُوَ عَلَى كُلِّ شَىْءٍ قَدِيرٌ، لَا حَوْلَ وَلَا قُوَّةَ إِلَّا بِاللهِ، سُبْحَانَ اللهِ، وَالْحَمْدُ لِلهِ، وَلَا إِلَهَ إِلَّا اللهُ، وَاللهُ أَكْبَرُ

ابن السني : رقم الحديث ٧٢٠

**DAY 325**

### FOR FORGIVENESS

O Lord, forgive me and accept my repentance for indeed You are Most Forgiving, Most Relenting.

(AD/T)

**DAY 326**

### FOR FORGIVENESS

O Allah, forgive us, have mercy on us, be pleased with us, accept us, enter us into Paradise, save us from the Fire and correct all of our affairs.

(TbD)

**اليوم ٣٢٥**

للمغفرة

رَبِّ اغْفِرْ لِي وَتُبْ عَلَيَّ إِنَّكَ أَنْتَ التَّوَّابُ الْغَفُورُ

أبو داوود : كتاب الوتر/ ١٥١٦، الترمذي : كتاب الدعوات/ ٣٤٣٤

**اليوم ٣٢٦**

للمغفرة

اللَّهُمَّ اغْفِرْ لَنَا، وَارْحَمْنَا وَارْضَ عَنَّا، وَتَقَبَّلْ مِنَّا، وَأَدْخِلْنَا الْجَنَّةَ، وَنَجِّنَا مِنَ النَّارِ، وَأَصْلِحْ لَنَا شَأْنَنَا كُلَّهُ

الدعاء للطبراني : رقم الحديث ١٤٤٢

### For forgiveness

O Allah, unite our hearts, reconcile our differences, guide us to the paths of peace, save us [by taking us] from darkness to the light, make us avoid indecency that is obvious and that is hidden, bless us in our hearing, sight, hearts, spouses and offspring and relent for You are indeed Oft-Relenting.

(AD)

### For forgiveness

O Allah, I ask You, O Allah, the One, the Everlasting Refuge, Who has not begotten, nor has been begotten, to Whom no one is equal, to forgive my sins, for indeed You are Forgiving and Merciful.

(AD/TbD)

**للمغفرة**

اللَّهُمَّ أَلِّفْ بَيْنَ قُلُوبِنَا وَأَصْلِحْ ذَاتَ بَيْنِنَا وَاهْدِنَا سُبُلَ
السَّلَامِ وَنَجِّنَا مِنَ الظُّلُمَاتِ إِلَى النُّورِ وَجَنِّبْنَا الْفَوَاحِشَ
مَا ظَهَرَ مِنْهَا وَمَا بَطَنَ وَبَارِكْ لَنَا فِى أَسْمَاعِنَا وَأَبْصَارِنَا
وَقُلُوبِنَا وَأَزْوَاجِنَا وَذُرِّيَّاتِنَا وَتُبْ عَلَيْنَا إِنَّكَ أَنْتَ التَّوَّابُ

أبو داوود : كتاب الصلاة/ ٩٦٩

**للمغفرة**

اللَّهُمَّ إِنِّى أَسْأَلُكَ يَا اللهُ الْأَحَدُ الصَّمَدُ، الَّذِى لَمْ يَلِدْ وَلَمْ
يُولَدْ، وَلَمْ يَكُنْ لَهُ كُفُوًا أَحَدٌ، أَنْ تَغْفِرَ لِى ذُنُوبِى، إِنَّكَ أَنْتَ
الْغَفُورُ الرَّحِيمُ

أبو داوود: كتاب الصلاة/ ٩٨٥ ، الدعاء للطبراني : رقم الحديث ٦١٦

### For a good end

O Allah, make my last days the best of my life; the best of my works those that I perform at the end of my life; and make the very best of my days the day I meet You.

(IS)

### For protection against Hellfire

You Whose forgiveness is great, O You Who is excellent in overlooking faults, O You Whose forgiveness is expansive, O You Who extends His Hands with mercy, O You to Whom all entreaties are directed, O You to Whom all complaints end up, O Generous in forgiving, O You Who are tremendous in bestowing favours, O You Who initiates blessings even before anyone deserves them, O our Lord, O our Master, O our Utmost Goal, I ask You, O Allah, not to roast my form in the Fire.

(H)

لحسن الخاتمة

اللَّهُمَّ اجْعَلْ خَيْرَ عُمْرِى ءاخِرَهُ، وَخَيْرَ عَمَلِى خَوَاتِمَهُ،
وَاجْعَلْ خَيْرَ أَيَّامِى يَوْمَ أَلْقَاكَ

ابن السني : رقم الحديث ١٢١

للتعوذ من النار

يَا عَظِيمَ الْعُفْوِ، يَا حَسَنَ التَّجَاوُزِ، يَا وَاسِعَ الْمَغْفِرَةِ، يَا بَاسِطَ
الْيَدَيْنِ بِالرَّحْمَةِ، يَا صَاحِبَ كُلِّ نَجْوَى، وَيَا مُنْتَهَى كُلِّ
شَكْوَى، يَا كَرِيمَ الصَّفْحِ، يَا عَظِيمَ الْمَنِّ، يَا مُبْتَدِئَ النِّعَمِ
قَبْلَ اسْتِحْقَاقِهَا، يَا رَبَّنَا، وَيَا سَيِّدَنَا، وَيَا مَوْلَانَا، وَيَا غَايَةَ
رَغْبَتِنَا، أَسْأَلُكَ يَا اللَّهَ أَنْ لَا تَشْوِى خَلْقِى بِالنَّارِ

المستدرك : رقم الحديث ٢٠٥٠

### FOR PROTECTION AGAINST HELLFIRE

*O* Allah, I seek refuge in You from the Fire.

(T)

### TO ASK FOR PARADISE

*O* Allah, I ask of You the Garden.

(T)

**اليوم ٣٣١**

للتعوذ من النار

اَللَّهُمَّ إِنِّى أَسْتَجِيْرُكَ مِنَ النَّارِ

الترمذي : كتاب صفة الجنة/ ٢٥٧٢

**اليوم ٣٣٢**

لطلب الجنة

اَللَّهُمَّ إِنِّى أَسْأَلُكَ الْجَنَّةَ

الترمذي : كتاب صفة الجنة/ ٢٥٧٢

### A GENERAL PRAYER

O Allah, Creator of the heavens and earth, Knower of the visible world and of the unseen, Lord of all things and their Master, I bear witness that there is no god except You, alone without partners, and I bear witness that Muhammad is Your slave and Messenger; I seek refuge in You from incurring a transgression or cause it to happen to another Muslim.

(TbD)

### A GENERAL PRAYER

O Light of the heavens and earth, O Conqueror of the heavens and earth, O Possessor of majesty and beneficence, O You towards Whom the cries of help of those who beseech Your aid are directed, O Helper of those who seek help, O Ultimate End of the desires of those who have desires, O Remover of

دُعاء عام

اللَّهُمَّ فاطِرَ السَّمَواتِ وَالْأَرْضِ، عَالِمَ الْغَيْبِ وَالشَّهَادَةِ، رَبَّ كُلِّ شَيْءٍ وَمَلِيكَهُ، أَشْهَدُ أَنْ لَا إِلَهَ إِلَّا أَنْتَ، وَحْدَكَ لَا شَرِيكَ لَكَ، وَأَشْهَدُ أَنَّ مُحَمَّدًا عَبْدُكَ وَرَسُولُكَ، أَعُوذُ بِكَ أَنْ أَقْتَرِفَ عَلَى نَفْسِى سَيِّئَةً أَوْ أَجُرَّهَا إِلَى مُسْلِمٍ

الدعاء للطبراني/ رقم الحديث: ١٤٥٦

دُعاء عام

يَا نُورَ السَّمَواتِ وَالْأَرْضِ، وَيَا جَبَّارَ السَّمَواتِ وَالْأَرْضِ، وَيَا ذَا الْجَلَالِ وَالْإِكْرَامِ، وَيَا صَرِيخَ الْمُسْتَصْرِخِينَ، وَيَا غَوْثَ الْمُسْتَغِيثِينَ، وَيَا مُنْتَهَى رَغْبَةِ الرَّاغِبِينَ،

afflictions, O Appeaser of those who have worries, O You Who answers the supplications of those under duress, O You Who clears away evil, O Most Merciful of those that have mercy and God of all the world, to You we address all our needs.

(TbD)

### DAY 335

#### A GENERAL PRAYER

O Allah, I ask You for guidance, Godfearingness, virtuousness and contentment.

(M/T)

وَالْمُفَرِّجُ عَنِ الْمَكْرُوبِينَ، وَالْمُرَوِّحُ عَنِ الْمَغْمُومِينَ، وَمُجِيبَ دَعْوَةِ الْمُضْطَرِّينَ، وَكَاشِفَ السُّوءِ وَأَرْحَمَ الرَّاحِمِينَ، وَإِلَهَ الْعَالَمِينَ نُنْزِلُ بِكَ كُلَّ حَاجَةٍ

الدعاء للطبراني/ رقم الحديث: ١٤٥٩

اليوم
٣٣٥

دعاء عام

اللَّهُمَّ إِنِّي أَسْأَلُكَ الْهُدَى وَالتُّقَى وَالْعَفَافَ وَالْغِنَى

مسلم: كتاب الذكر والدعاء/ ٢٧٢١، الترمذي: كتاب الدعوات/ ٣٤٨٩

**DAY**
**336**

### A general prayer

O Allah, guide me and direct me to the correct course of action.

(M)

**DAY**
**337**

### A general prayer

O Allah, forgive me, have mercy on me, grant me well-being and provide me with sustenance.

(M)

دعاء عام

اَللَّهُمَّ اهْدِنِيْ وَسَدِّدْنِيْ

مسلم: كتاب الذكر والدعاء/ ٢٧٢٥

دعاء عام

اللَّهُمَّ اغْفِرْ لِيْ وَارْحَمْنِيْ وَعَافِنِيْ وَارْزُقْنِيْ

مسلم: كتاب الذّكر والدعاء/ ٢٦٩٧

### DAY 338

#### A GENERAL PRAYER

O Allah, I ask You a righteous living, a good end and a return that is neither disgraceful nor shameful.

(TbD)

### DAY 339

#### A GENERAL PRAYER

O Allah, show me what is best and choose it for me.

(IS)

دعاء عام

اللَّهُمَّ إِنِّي أَسْأَلُكَ عِيشَةً تَقِيَّةً، وَمِيتَةً سَوِيَّةً، وَمَرَدًّا غَيْرَ مُخْزٍ وَلَا فَاضِحٍ

الدعاء للطبراني/ رقم الحديث ١٤٣٥

دعاء عام

اللَّهُمَّ خِرْ لِي وَاخْتَرْ لِي

ابن السني : رقم الحديث ٥٩٧

**DAY**
**340**

O Allah, You are peace and from You is peace, so make us live, O our Lord, by peace.

(IAS)

**DAY**
**341**

A GENERAL PRAYER

O Allah, make me of those who expect glad tidings when they do good, and seek forgiveness when they transgress.

(TbD)

دعاء عام

اللَّهُمَّ أَنْتَ السَّلَامُ، وَمِنْكَ السَّلَامُ، فَحَيِّنَا رَبَّنَا بِالسَّلَامِ

مصنف ابن أبي شيبة : رقم الحديث ٢٩٦٢٥

دعاء عام

اللَّهُمَّ اجْعَلْنِي مِنَ الَّذِينَ إِذَا أَحْسَنُوا اسْتَبْشَرُوا، وَإِذَا
أَسَاءُوا اسْتَغْفَرُوا

الدعاء للطبراني/ رقم الحديث : ١٤٠١

### A GENERAL PRAYER

O Allah, I ask for Your pardon and for well-being.

(T)

### A GENERAL PRAYER

Lord, I ask You for well-being and safety in this world and in the next.

(T)

دعاء عام

اَللَّهُمَّ إِنِّيْ أَسْأَلُكَ الْعَفْوَ وَالْعَافِيَةَ

الترمذي : كتاب الدعوات/ ٣٥٥٨

دعاء عام

رَبِّ إِنِّيْ أَسْأَلُكَ الْعَافِيَةَ وَالمُعَافَاةَ فِى الدُّنْيَا وَالْأَخِرَةِ

الترمذي : كتاب الدعوات/ ٣٥١٢

DAY
**344**

### A GENERAL PRAYER

O Allah, give us more, not less, honour us and do not humiliate us, give to us and do not deprive us, prefer us and do not prefer others over us, make us pleased and be pleased with us.

(T)

DAY
**345**

### A GENERAL PRAYER

O Allah, I ask You for Your love, the love of whoever loves You, and the love of any work that will get me to love You; O Allah, make it so that Your love is more beloved to me than my own self, family and cold water.

(T)

دعاء عام

اللَّهُمَّ زِدْنَا وَلاَ تَنْقُصْنَا وَأَكْرِمْنَا وَلاَ تُهِنَّا وَأَعْطِنَا
وَلاَ تَحْرِمْنَا وَءَاثِرْنَا وَلاَ تُؤْثِرْ عَلَيْنَا وَأَرْضِنَا وَارْضَ عَنَّا

الترمذي : كتاب تفسير القرآن/ ٣١٧٣

دعاء عام

اللَّهُمَّ إِنِّي أَسْأَلُكَ حُبَّكَ وَحُبَّ مَنْ يُحِبُّكَ وَالْعَمَلَ الَّذِى
يُبَلِّغُنِي حُبَّكَ اللَّهُمَّ اجْعَلْ حُبَّكَ أَحَبَّ إِلَيَّ مِنْ نَفْسِى
وَأَهْلِى وَمِنَ الْمَاءِ الْبَارِدِ

الترمذي : كتاب الدعوات/ ٣٤٩٠

### DAY 346

O Allah, enable me to magnify Your praise, to remember You in abundance, to follow Your admonition and to preserve Your injunction.

(A)

### DAY 347

O Allah, make my inner being better than my outward being and make my outward being righteous. O Allah, I ask You for the best of what You grant people of wealth, family and offspring, that is neither misguided nor misguiding.

(T)

دعاء عام

اللَّهُمَّ اجْعَلْنِي أُعْظِمُ شُكْرَكَ وَأُكْثِرُ ذِكْرَكَ وَأَتَّبِعُ نَصِيحَتَكَ وَأَحْفَظُ وَصِيَّتَكَ

أحمد : رقم الحديث ٨١٠١

دعاء عام

اللَّهُمَّ اجْعَلْ سَرِيرَتِي خَيْرًا مِنْ عَلَانِيَتِي وَاجْعَلْ عَلَانِيَتِي صَالِحَةً اللَّهُمَّ إِنِّي أَسْأَلُكَ مِنْ صَالِحِ مَا تُؤْتِي النَّاسَ مِنَ الْمَالِ وَالْأَهْلِ وَالْوَلَدِ غَيْرِ الضَّالِّ وَلَا الْمُضِلِّ

الترمذي : كتاب الدعوات/ ٣٥٨٦

### A GENERAL PRAYER

O Allah, I ask You for all good that is immediate and is deferred, that which I know of and that which I do not; and I seek refuge in You from all evil, both immediate and deferred, that which I know of and that which I do not. O Allah, I ask You for that which Your slave and Prophet asked You for, and I seek refuge in You from that which Your slave and Prophet sought refuge from in You. And I ask of You Paradise and that which brings [me] closer to it, of speech or action, and I seek refuge in You from the Fire and that which brings [me] closer to it, of speech or action; and I ask You to make every decree of Yours good for me.

(TbD/IAS)

دعاء عام

اللَّهُمَّ إِنِّي أَسْأَلُكَ مِنَ الْخَيْرِ كُلِّهِ عَاجِلِهِ وَءَاجِلِهِ مَا عَلِمْتُ
مِنْهُ وَمَا لَمْ أَعْلَمْ، وَأَعُوذُ بِكَ مِنَ الشَّرِّ كُلِّهِ عَاجِلِهِ وَءَاجِلِهِ
مَا عَلِمْتُ مِنْهُ وَمَا لَمْ أَعْلَمْ، اللَّهُمَّ إِنِّي أَسْأَلُكَ مِمَّا سَأَلَكَ
عَبْدُكَ وَنَبِيُّكَ، وَأَعُوذُ بِكَ مِمَّا عَاذَ مِنْهُ عَبْدُكَ وَنَبِيُّكَ،
وَأَسْأَلُكَ الْجَنَّةَ وَمَا قَرَّبَ إِلَيْهَا مِنْ قَوْلٍ أَوْ عَمَلٍ، وَأَعُوذُ
بِكَ مِنَ النَّارِ وَمَا قَرَّبَ إِلَيْهَا مِنْ قَوْلٍ أَوْ عَمَلٍ، وَأَسْأَلُكَ
أَنْ تَجْعَلَ كُلَّ قَضَاءٍ تَقْضِيهِ لِي خَيْرًا

الدعاء للطبراني : رقم الحديث ١٣٤٧ ، ابن أبي شيبة : رقم الحديث ٢٩٣٤٥

### A GENERAL PRAYER

In the name of Allah apart from Whom there is no god, the Merciful the Compassionate; O Allah remove worry and anxiety from me.

(TbMK)

### A GENERAL PRAYER

There is no god except Allah and Allah is great; there is no god except Allah, alone without partners; there is no god except Allah, to Him belongs the dominion and praise; there is no god except Allah, and there is no strength or power except through Allah.

(T)

دعاء عام

بِسْمِ اللهِ الَّذِي لَا إِلَهَ إِلاَّ هُوَ الرَّحْمَنُ الرَّحِيمُ، اللَّهُمَّ أَذْهِبْ
عَنِّي الْهَمَّ وَالْحَزَنَ

الدعاء للطبراني : رقم الحديث ٦٥٩

دعاء عام

لَا إِلَهَ إِلاَّ اللهُ وَاللهُ أَكْبَرُ لاَ إِلَهَ إِلاَّ اللهُ وَحْدَهُ لاَ إِلَهَ
إِلاَّ اللهُ وَحْدَهُ لاَ شَرِيكَ لَهُ لاَ إِلَهَ إِلاَّ اللهُ لَهُ الْمُلْكُ وَلَهُ
الْحَمْدُ لاَ إِلَهَ إِلاَّ اللهُ وَلاَ حَوْلَ وَلاَ قُوَّةَ إِلاَّ بِاللهِ

الترمذي : كتاب الدعوات/ ٣٤٣٠

### DAY
### 351

#### A GENERAL PRAYER

O Allah, I ask You for health accompanied by faith, for faith accompanied with good manners, for safety followed with success and for mercy from You along with well-being, and for forgiveness from You and Your good pleasure.

(H)

### DAY
### 352

#### A GENERAL PRAYER

O Allah, make good the end of all our matters and protect us from the wretchedness of this world and from the chastisement of the hereafter.

(TbD)

اليوم
٣٥١

دعاء عام

اللَّهُمَّ إِنِّي أَسْأَلُكَ صِحَّةً فِي إِيمَانٍ، وَإِيمَانًا فِي حُسْنِ خُلُقٍ، وَنَجَاةً يَتْبَعُهَا فَلَاحٌ وَرَحْمَةً مِنْكَ، وَعَافِيَةً وَمَغْفِرَةً مِنْكَ وَرِضْوَانًا

المستدرك: ١٩٧١

اليوم
٣٥٢

دعاء عام

اللَّهُمَّ أَحْسِنْ عَاقِبَتَنَا فِي الْأُمُورِ كُلِّهَا، وَأَجِرْنَا مِنْ خِزْيِ الدُّنْيَا وَعَذَابِ الْآخِرَةِ

الدعاء للطبراني/ رقم الحديث: ١٤٣٦

### DAY 353

#### A GENERAL PRAYER

*O* Allah, I seek refuge in You from the cessation of Your blessings, the changing of the well-being You grant, from the suddenness of Your revenge and from all Your wrath.

(M/AD)

### DAY 354

#### A GENERAL PRAYER

*O* Allah, I seek refuge in You from the evil I committed and from the evil I did not commit.

(M)

اليوم
٣٥٣

دعاء عام

اللَّهُمَّ إِنِّي أَعُوذُ بِكَ مِنْ زَوَالِ نِعْمَتِكَ وَتَحَوُّلِ عَافِيَتِكَ
وَفُجَاءَةِ نِقْمَتِكَ وَجَمِيعِ سَخَطِكَ

مسلم: كتاب الرقاق/ ٢٧٣٩، أبو داوود: كتاب الوتر/ ١٥٤٥

اليوم
٣٥٤

دعاء عام

اللَّهُمَّ إِنِّي أَعُوذُ بِكَ مِنْ شَرِّ مَا عَمِلْتُ وَشَرِّ مَا لَمْ أَعْمَلْ

مسلم: كتاب الذّكر والدعاء/ ٢٧١٦

### DAY 355

A GENERAL PRAYER

O Allah, I seek refuge in You from the trial of the Fire and the chastisement of the Fire, from the trial of the grave and the chastisement of the grave, and from the evil trial of wealth and the evil trial of poverty; O Allah, I seek refuge in You from the evil trial of the false Messiah.

(B)

### DAY 356

A GENERAL PRAYER

O Allah, I seek refuge in Your good pleasure from Your wrath and in Your protection from Your punishment; and I seek refuge in You from You, [and] I cannot praise You as You have praised Yourself.

(M)

دعاء عام

اللَّهُمَّ إِنِّي أَعُوذُ بِكَ مِنْ فِتْنَةِ النَّارِ وَعَذَابِ النَّارِ، وَفِتْنَةِ الْقَبْرِ وَعَذَابِ الْقَبْرِ وَشَرِّ فِتْنَةِ الْغِنَى، وَشَرِّ فِتْنَةِ الْفَقْرِ، اللَّهُمَّ إِنِّي أَعُوذُ بِكَ مِنْ شَرِّ فِتْنَةِ الْمَسِيحِ الدَّجَّالِ

البخاري : كتاب الدعوات/ ٦٣٧٦

دعاء عام

اللَّهُمَّ أَعُوذُ بِرِضَاكَ مِنْ سَخَطِكَ وَبِمُعَافَاتِكَ مِنْ عُقُوبَتِكَ وَأَعُوذُ بِكَ مِنْكَ لَا أُحْصِي ثَنَاءً عَلَيْكَ أَنْتَ كَمَا أَثْنَيْتَ عَلَى نَفْسِكَ

مسلم : كتاب الصلاة/ ٤٨٦

### DAY 357

A GENERAL PRAYER

O Allah, make me avoid the most despicable manners, works, whims and diseases.

(TbD)

### DAY 358

A GENERAL PRAYER

O Allah, I seek refuge in You from the strain of tribulation, from being overtaken by wretchedness, from the evil of things decreed and from the spitefulness of enemies.

(B)

**اليوم ٣٥٧**

دعاء عام

اللَّهُمَّ جَنِّبْنِي مُنْكَرَاتِ الْأَخْلَاقِ وَالْأَعْمَالِ وَالْأَهْوَاءِ وَالْأَدْوَاءِ

الدعاء للطبراني : رقم الحديث ١٣٨٤

**اليوم ٣٥٨**

دعاء عام

اللَّهُمَّ إِنِّي أَعُوذُ بِكَ مِنْ جَهْدِ الْبَلَاءِ، وَدَرَكِ الشَّقَاءِ، وَسُوءِ الْقَضَاءِ، وَشَمَاتَةِ الْأَعْدَاءِ

البخاري : كتاب الدعوات/ ٦٣٤٧

## DAY 359

O Allah, forgive me, have mercy on me, guide me and provide for me.

(M)

## DAY 360

A GENERAL PRAYER

O Allah, correct for me my religion in which lies the safeguarding of my whole matter; and correct for me my worldly life in which lies my livelihood; and correct for me my afterlife in which lies my return; and make life an increase for me in everything that is good, and make death for me a repose from all that is evil.

(M)

دعاء عام

اللَّهُمَّ اغْفِرْ لِي وَارْحَمْنِي وَاهْدِنِي وَارْزُقْنِي

مسلم : كتاب الذكر و الدعاء/ ٢٦٩٧

دعاء عام

اللَّهُمَّ أَصْلِحْ لِي دِينِيَ الَّذِي هُوَ عِصْمَةُ أَمْرِي وَأَصْلِحْ لِي
دُنْيَايَ الَّتِي فِيهَا مَعَاشِي وَأَصْلِحْ لِي ءَاخِرَتِي الَّتِي فِيهَا
مَعَادِي وَاجْعَلِ الْحَيَاةَ زِيَادَةً لِي فِي كُلِّ خَيْرٍ وَاجْعَلِ الْمَوْتَ
رَاحَةً لِي مِنْ كُلِّ شَرٍّ

مسلم : كتاب الذكر والدعاء/ ٢٧٢٠

DAY
**361**

### A general prayer

O Allah, conceal my faults and appease my fears.

(AD)

DAY
**362**

### A general prayer

O Allah, I ask You for pardon and well-being in my religion, my worldly life, my family and my wealth.

(AD)

اليوم
٣٦١

دعاء عام

اللَّهُمَّ اسْتُرْ عَوْرَاتِي وَءَامِنْ رَوْعَاتِي

أبو داوود: كتاب الأدب/ ٥٠٧٣

اليوم
٣٦٢

دعاء عام

اللَّهُمَّ إِنِّي أَسْأَلُكَ الْعَفْوَ وَالْعَافِيَةَ فِي دِينِي وَدُنْيَايَ وَأَهْلِي وَمَالِي

أبو داوود: كتاب الأدب/ ٥٠٧٤

**DAY 363**

### A GENERAL PRAYER

*O* Allah, inspire in me good sense and protect me from the evil of my own self.

(T)

**DAY 364**

### A GENERAL PRAYER

*O* Allah, benefit me by what You have taught me, teach me what benefits me and provide me with knowledge that benefits me.

(TbD)

دعاء عام

اللَّهُمَّ أَلْهِمْنِي رُشْدِى وَأَعِذْنِي مِنْ شَرِّ نَفْسِى

الترمذي: كتاب الدعوات/ ٣٤٨٣

دعاء عام

اللَّهُمَّ انْفَعْنِي بِمَا عَلَّمْتَنِي، وَعَلِّمْنِي مَا يَنْفَعُنِي، وَارْزُقْنِي عِلْمًا تَنْفَعُنِي بِهِ

الدعاء للطبراني: رقم الحديث ١٤٠٥

### DAY 365

A GENERAL PRAYER

O Allah, make me content with what You have provided me, bless me in it and bestow good upon all that is out of my sight.

(B)

### DAY 366

A GENERAL PRAYER

O Allah, enable me to enjoy my hearing and sight and make that I fully enjoy them for as long as I live, support me against him who wrongs me, and take revenge against him on my behalf.

(T)

دعاء عام

اللَّهُمَّ قَنِّعْنِي بِمَا رَزَقْتَنِي، وَبَارِكْ لِي فِيهِ، وَاخْلُفْ عَلَى كُلَّ
غَائِبَةٍ بِخَيْرٍ

البخاري : الأدب المفرد/ رقم الحديث ٧٠٢

دعاء عام

اللَّهُمَّ مَتِّعْنِي بِسَمْعِي وَبَصَرِي وَاجْعَلْهُمَا الْوَارِثَ مِنِّي
وَانْصُرْنِي عَلَى مَنْ يَظْلِمُنِي وَخُذْ مِنْهُ بِثَأْرِي

الترمذي : كتاب الدعوات/ ٣٦١١

# BIBLIOGRAPHY

Abu Dawud, Sulayman, *Sunan Abi Dawud*, ed. Muhammad Muhyi al-Din 'Abd al-Hamid (Damascus: Dar al-Fikr, n.d.). [= AD]

Al-Bukhari, Muhammad ibn Isma'il, *Al-Adab al-mufrad*, ed. Khalid al-'Akk (Lahore: Maktabah Rahmaniyah, 1415H). [= BA]

Al-Bukhari, Muhammad ibn Isma'il, *Sahih al-Bukhari* (Damascus: Dar ibn Kathir, 2002). [= B]

Al-Hakim al-Nisaburi, Abu 'Abd Allah, *Al-Mustadrak 'ala al-Sahihayn*, ed. Muqbil al-Wadi'i (Cairo: Dar al-Haramayn, 1997). [= H]

Al-Haythami, Abu al-Hasan, *Majma' al-Zawa'id wa manba' al-fawa'id*, ed. Husam al-Din al-Qudsi (Cairo: Maktabah al-Qudsi, 1994). [= Hy]

Ibn Abu Shaybah, 'Abd al-Rahman, *Al-Musannaf fi al-ahadith wa al-adhkar*, ed. Kamal Yusuf al-Hut (Riyadh: Maktabah al-Rushd, 1409H). [= IAS]

Ibn al-Hujjaj, Muslim, *Sahih Muslim*, ed. by al-Fariyabi (Riyadh: Dar al-Tayyibah, 2006). [= M]

Ibn al-Sunni, Ahmad, *'Amal al-yawm wa al-laylah*, ed. Muhammad 'Uyun (Damascus: Dar al-Bayan, 1407H). [= IS]

Ibn Hanbal, Ahmad, *Al-Musnad*, ed. Shu'ayb al-Arna'ut (Mu'asasah al-Risalah, 2001H). [= A]

Ibn Majah, Muhammad, *Sunan Ibn Majah*, ed. Muhammad Mustafa al-'Azami (Riyadh: Sharikah al-Tiba'ah al-'Arabiyah al-Su'udiyah, 1984). [= IM]

Al-Mundhiri, 'Abd al-'Azim, *Al-Targhib wa al-tarhib*, ed. Ibrahim Shams al-Din (Beirut: Dar al-Kutub al-'Ilmiyyah, 1417). [= TT]

Al-Nawawi, Muhyi al-Din, *Al-Adhkar*, ed. 'Abd al-Qadir al-Arna'ut (Damascus: Dar al-Mallah, 1971). [= N]

Al-Shawkani, Muhammad, *Nayl al-awtar*, ed. 'Isam al-Din al-Sababti (Egypt: Dar al-Hadith, 1993).  [= S]

Al-Tabarani, Abu al-Qasim, *Al-Mu'jam al-awsat*, ed. Tariq Muhammad and 'Abd al-Muhsin al-Husayni (Cairo: Dar al-Haramayn, 1415H). [= TbMA]

Al-Tabarani, Abu al-Qasim, *Al-Mu'jam al-kabir*, ed. Hamdi al-Salafi (Beirut: Dar Ihya' al-Turath al-'Arabiyah, 2002). [= TbMK]

Al-Tabarani, Abu al-Qasim, *Du'a'*, ed. Muhammad Sa'id al-Bukhari (Beirut: Dar al-Basha>ir al-Islamiyah, 1987). [=TbD]

Al-Tirmidhi, Abu 'Isa, *Sunan al-Tirmidhi*, ed. Ahmad Shakir (Egypt: Matba'ah al-Halabi, 1978). [= T]

# المـراجـع

ابن أبي شيبة، عبد الله، المصنف في الأحاديث والآثار، المحقق: كمال يوسف الحوت، ١٤٠٩ هـ، ط ١، مكتبة الرشد، الرياض

ابن الحجاج، مسلم، صحيح مسلم، تحقيق الفاريابي، ط ١، ٢٠٠٦، دار طيبة، الرياض

ابن السني، أحمد، عمل اليوم والليلة، تحقيق محمد عيون، ط ١، ١٤٠٧ هـ، دار البيان، دمشق

ابن حنبل، أحمد، المسند، تحقيق شعيب الأرناؤوط، ط ١، ٢٠٠١، مؤسسة الرسالة

ابن ماجه، محمد، سنن ابن ماجه، تحقيق محمد مصطفى الاعظمي، ١٩٨٤، ط ٢، شركة الطباعة العربية السعودية، الرياض

أبو داوود، سليمان، سنن أبي داوود، تحقيق محمد محيي الدين عبد الحميد، دار الفكر، دمشق

البخاري، محمد بن إسماعيل، الأدب المفرد، تحقيق خالد العك، ١٤١٥ هجري، مكتبة رحمانية، لاهور

———، صحيح البخاري، ط ١، ٢٠٠٢، دار ابن كثير، دمشق

الترمذي، أبو عيسى، سنن الترمذي، تحقيق أحمد شاكر، ط ٢،
١٩٧٨، مطبعة الحلبي، مصر

الحاكم النيسابوري، أبو عبد الله، المستدرك على الصحيحين، تحقيق
مقبل الوادعي، ١٩٩٧، ط ١، دار الحرمين، القاهرة

الشوكاني، محمد، نيل الأوطار، تحقيق: عصام الدين الصبابطي،
١٩٩٣، دار الحديث، مصر الطبعة :الأولى

الطبراني، أبو القاسم، الدعاء، تحقيق: محمد سعيد البخاري، ط ١،
١٩٨٧، دار البشائر الإسلامية، بيروت

ـــــــ، المعجم الأوسط، تحقيق طارق محمد وعبد المحسن
الحسيني، ١٤١٥ هـ، دار الحرمين، القاهرة

ـــــــ، المعجم الكبير، تحقيق حمدي السلفي، ٢٠٠٢، طبعة ٢،
دار احياء التراث العربي، بيروت

المنذري، عبد العظيم، الترغيب والترهيب، المحقق :إبراهيم شمس
الدين، ١٤١٧، ط ١، دار الكتب العلمية – بيروت

النووي، محيي الدين، الأذكار، تحقيق عبد القادر الأرناؤوط، ١٩٧١،
دار الملاح، دمشق

الهيثمي، أبو الحسن، مجمع الزوائد ومنبع الفوائد، تحقيق حسام الدين
القدسي، ١٩٩٤، مكتبة القدسي، القاهرة

# INDEX

Note: Reference is made in this index to where the English terms appear according to the page numbers; Arabic translations are on the facing pages.